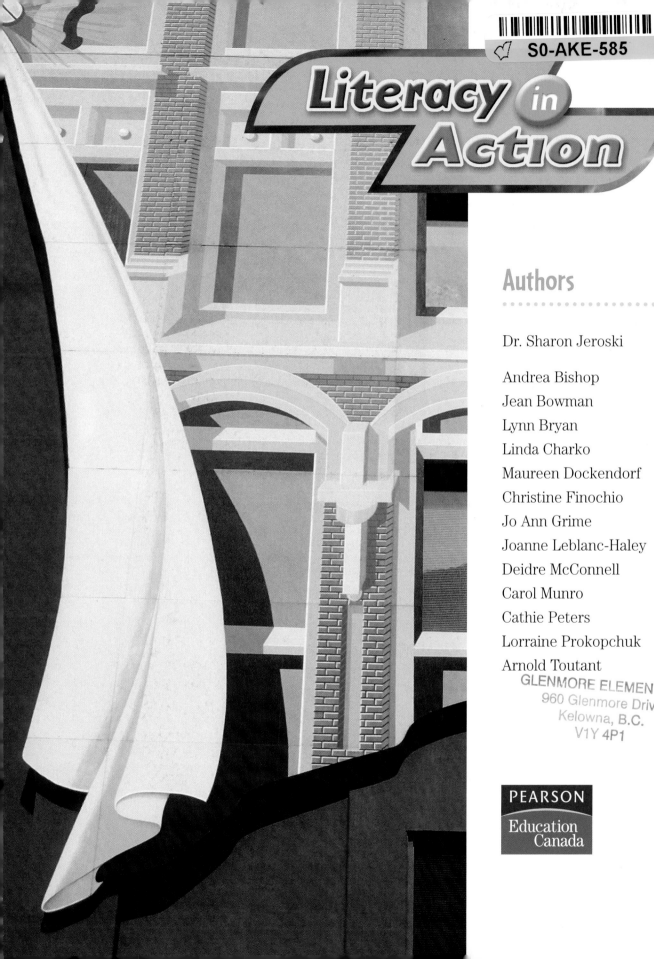

Literacy in Action

Authors

Dr. Sharon Jeroski

Andrea Bishop
Jean Bowman
Lynn Bryan
Linda Charko
Maureen Dockendorf
Christine Finochio
Jo Ann Grime
Joanne Leblanc-Haley
Deidre McConnell
Carol Munro
Cathie Peters
Lorraine Prokopchuk
Arnold Toutant

PEARSON

Education
Canada

This book is dedicated to the memory of Iris Zammit, whose passion for learning inspired everyone who worked with her.

Grade 6 Project Team

Team Leader and Publisher: Anita Borovilos
National Literacy Consultants: Beth Ecclestone and Norma MacFarlane
Publishers: Susan Green and Elynor Kagan
Product Managers: Donna Neumann, Paula Smith
Managing Editor: Monica Schwalbe
Developmental Editors: Chelsea Donaldson, Elaine Gareau, and Mariangela Gentile
Production Editors: Susan Ginsberg, Milena Mazzolin, Adele Reynolds, and Lisa Santilli
Copy Editor: Jessica Westhead
Proofreaders: Rebecca Vogan and Jessica Westhead
Research: Glen Herbert and Rebecca Vogan
Production Coordinators: Donna Brown, Alison Dale, and Zane Kaneps
Senior Manufacturing Coordinator: Jane Schell
Art Director: Zena Denchik
Designers: Zena Denchik, Maki Ikushima, Anthony Leung, Alex Li, Carolyn Sebestyen, and Word & Image Design
Permissions Research: Cindy Howard
Photo Research: Glen Herbert, Amanda McCormick, and Grace O'Connell
Storyboard Posters: Barbara Boate and Deborah Kekewich
Vice-President Publishing and Marketing: Mark Cobham

Copyright © 2008 Pearson Education Canada, a division of Pearson Canada Inc., Toronto, Ontario

ISBN-13: 978-0-13-204742-5 (softcover)
ISBN-10: 0-13-204742-X (softcover)
ISBN-13: 978-0-13-204741-8 (hardcover)
ISBN-10: 0-13-204741-1 (hardcover)

Printed and bound in Canada.
3 4 5 TC 11 10 09

The publisher has taken every care to meet or exceed industry specifications for the manufacture of textbooks. The cover of this sewn book is a premium, polymer-reinforced material designed to provide long life and withstand rugged use. Mylar gloss lamination has been applied for further durability.

PEARSON
Education
Canada

Acknowledgements

Series Consultants

Andrea Bishop
Anne Boyd
Christine Finochio
Don Jones

Joanne Leblanc-Haley
Jill Maar
Joanne Rowlandson
Carole Stickley

Specialist Reviewers

Science: Doug Herridge
  Toronto, ON
Social Studies: Marg Lysecki
  Toronto, ON
Aboriginal: Ken Ealey
  Edmonton, AB

Equity: Dianna Mezzarobba
  Vancouver, BC
Levelling: Susan Pleli
  Stoney Creek, ON
Iris Zammit
  Toronto, ON

Grades 3–6 Advisors and Reviewers

Dr. Frank Serafini
  Assistant Professor,
  University of Las Vegas,
  Las Vegas, Nevada

Patricia Adamson
  Winnipeg, MB
Marion Ahrens
  Richmond Hill, ON
Ray Appel
  Vancouver, BC
Sandra Ball
  Surrey, BC
Gwen Bartnik
  Vancouver, BC
Jennifer Batycky
  Calgary, AB
Michelle Bellavia
  Hamilton, ON
Mary-Jane Black
  Hamilton, ON
Jackie Bradley
  Saskatoon, SK
Diane Campbell
  Durham, ON
Nancy Carl
  Coquitlam, BC
Janet Chow
  Burnaby, BC
Marla Ciccotelli
  London, ON
Susan Clarke
  Burlington, ON
Norma Collinson
  Truro, NS
Lynn Crews
  Lower Sackville, NS
Kathyrn D'Angelo
  Richmond, BC

Pat Dooley
  Nelson, BC
Susan Elliott
  Toronto, ON
Diane Gagley
  Calgary, AB
Michael Gallant
  Calgary, AB
Jennifer Gardner
  Vernon, BC
Adrienne Gear
  Vancouver, BC
Faye Gertz
  Niska, AB
Cindy Gordon
  Victoria, BC
James Gray
  Winnipeg, MB
Kathleen Gregory
  Victoria, BC
Myrtis Guy
  Torbay, NL
Kim Guyette-Carter
  Dartmouth, NS
Jackie Hall
  Vancouver, BC
Natalie Harnum
  Berwick, NS
Sherida Hassanali
  Herring Cove, NS
Deborah Holley
  Duncan, BC
Joanne Holme
  Surrey, BC
Patricia Horstead
  Maple Ridge, BC
Carol Hryniuk-Adamov
  Winnipeg, MB
Pamela Jacob
  Limestone, ON

Joanne Keller
  Delta, BC
Dawn Kesslering
  Regina, SK
Karen Quan King
  Toronto, ON
Linda Kirby
  Sault Ste. Marie, ON
Sheryl Koers
  Duncan, BC
Roger Lacey
  Calgary, AB
Sharon LeClair
  Coquitlam, BC
Catherine Little
  Toronto, ON
Caroline Lutyk
  Burlington, ON
Heather MacKay
  Richmond, BC
Margaret Marion
  Niagara Falls, ON
Sangeeta McAuley
  Toronto, ON
Paula McIntee
  Allanburg, ON
Caroline Mitchell
  Guelph, ON
Laura Mossey
  Durham, ON
Rhonda Nixon
  Edmonton, AB
Gillian Parsons
  Brantford, ON
Linda Perrin
  Saint John, NB
Charolette Player
  Edmonton, AB

Rhonda Rakimov
  Duncan, BC
Tammy Renyard
  Duncan, BC
Kristine Richards
  Windsor, ON
Kathryn Richmond
  St. Catharines, ON
Barbara Rushton
  New Minas, NS
Jaye Sawatsky
  Delta, BC
Michelle Sharratt
  Woodbridge, ON
Cathy Sheridan
  Ottawa, ON
Nanci-Jane Simpson
  Hamilton, ON
Kim Smith
  Newmarket, ON
Candace Spilsbury
  Duncan, BC
Sheila Staats
  Brantford, ON
Patricia Tapp
  Hamilton, ON
Vera Teschow
  Mississauga, ON
Joanne Traczuk
  Sutton West, ON
Sonja Willier
  Edmonton, AB
Susan Wilson
  St. Catharines, ON
Kelly Winney
  London, ON
Beth Zimmerman
  London, ON

CONTENTS

Independent Practice

Read! Write! Say! Do!

Your Literacy Portfolio

UNIT 5

Stories of Our Lives • 64

Read Together

Shared

Learn Together Poster

Guided Practice

Literacy in Action

Independent Practice

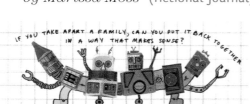

Read! Write! Say! Do!

Your Literacy Portfolio

Exploring Canada • 124

Read Together

Shared

Learn Together Poster

Guided Practice

Early Adventurers
  by Chelsea Donaldson (reports)

Literacy in Action

Independent Practice

Read! Write! Say! Do!

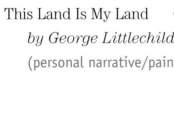

Your Literacy Portfolio

Arts and Entertainment

LEARNING GOALS

In this unit you will

- Read, view, and listen to opinions about arts and entertainment.

- Evaluate the ideas writers and designers present.

- Explore and share ideas through talk and visual representations.

- Create opinion articles and reviews for an entertainment magazine.

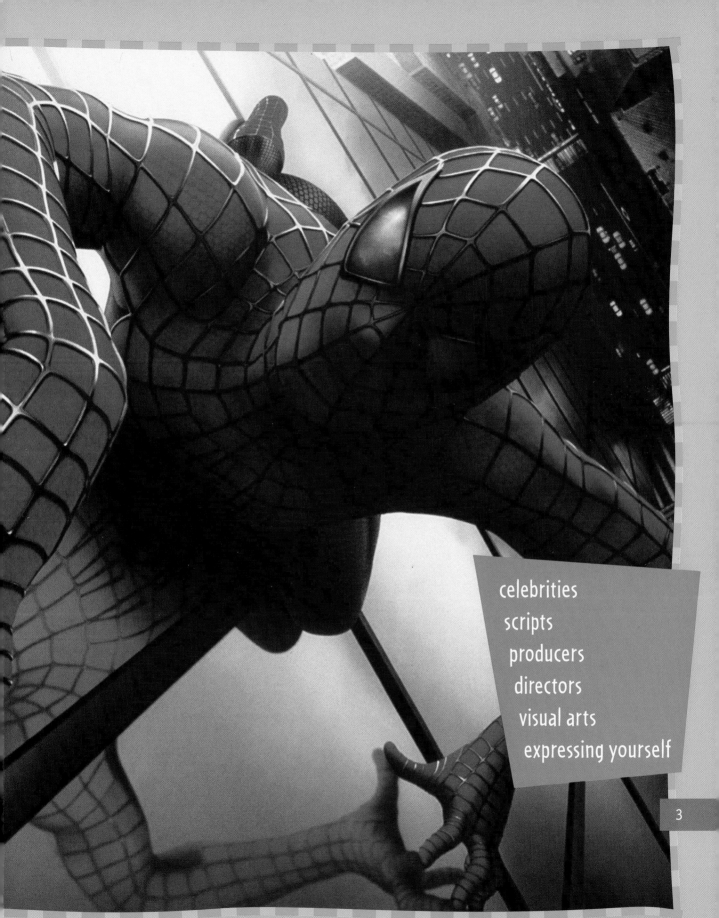

celebrities
scripts
producers
directors
visual arts
expressing yourself

What's Your Preference?

Illustrated by Dave Whamond

How do Grade 6
students like
to be entertained?

**What's your take on entertainment? Are you
a sports fan, a movie buff, a music maniac,
an art aficionado? Do you ever wonder what
other kids' entertainment interests are?**

There are so many different ways to be entertained. Answer the
questions in the survey to find out some of your preferences.
Then turn the page to compare your responses with those of
other Grade 6 students.

Entertainment Survey

1. Which **one** of the following types of music do you prefer?

    a) rap/hip hop
    b) classic rock
    c) alternative rock
    d) pop or Top 40
    e) metal

2. If you could attend **one** of the following events, which one would you choose?

    a) NHL hockey game
    b) music concert of your favourite singer
    c) skateboard competition
    d) entertainment awards show like the Junos or Oscars
    e) video game tournament

3. Which **one** of the following types of television shows do you enjoy most?

    a) reality shows
    b) sitcoms
    c) cartoon sitcoms
    d) dramas
    e) documentaries

4. If you could learn to do **one** of the following jobs in movies or television, which one would you choose?

    a) script writing
    b) directing (deciding on the scenes and guiding the actors)
    c) acting
    d) creating the music/soundtrack
    e) producing the commercials

5. If you could be **one** of the following visual artists, which one would you be?

    a) painter
    b) sculptor
    c) cartoonist
    d) computer animator
    e) photographer

RESULTS

The same survey was given to 100 girls and 100 boys in Grade 6 classrooms across Canada. Here are the results.

1. Which **one** of the following types of music do you prefer?

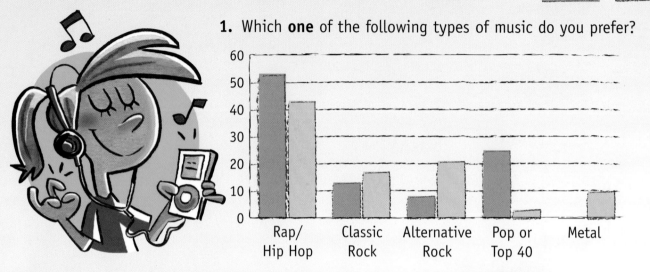

2. If you could attend **one** of the following events, which one would you choose?

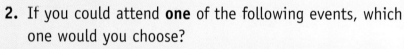

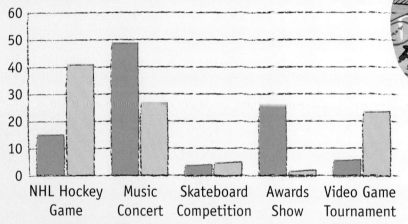

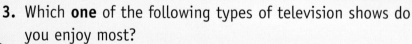

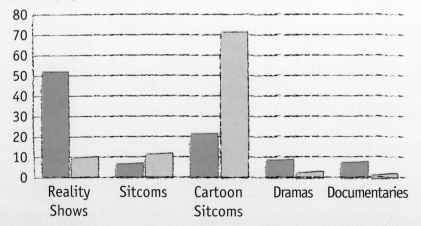

6

3. Which **one** of the following types of television shows do you enjoy most?

4. If you could learn to do **one** of the following jobs in movies or television, which one would you choose?

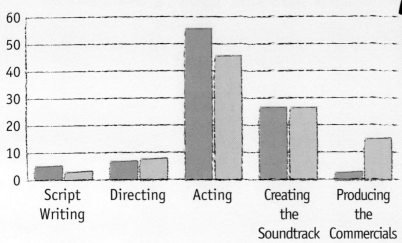

Script Writing | Directing | Acting | Creating the Soundtrack | Producing the Commercials

5. If you could be **one** of the following visual artists, which one would you be?

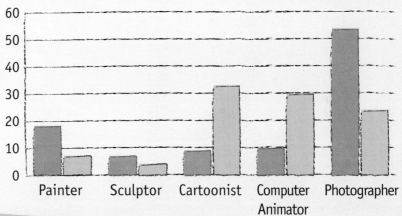

Painter | Sculptor | Cartoonist | Computer Animator | Photographer

LET'S TALK ABOUT IT...

• Meet with a group to talk about the results. What information do you get from each graph? When you look at all the results together, what general conclusions can you draw?

• In your group, think of a new survey question. Survey students in your grade and graph the results. Show your graph to the class and describe your findings.

Read Opinions and Editorials

Every day we hear and read other people's opinions in the media, on Web sites, and from friends and family. Opinions are everywhere!

TALK ABOUT IT!

Think of someone whose opinions interest you.

■ Who is it?

■ What are his or her opinions usually about?

■ Describe one opinion this person holds.

■ What reasons does he or she give to support this opinion?

Here are some places you can find opinions.

With a group, make a list of people who give opinions and where you hear them expressed.

People with opinions	Where the opinions are expressed
Sports commentators	Sports Talk Radio

Think Like a Reader

Read with a purpose

- Why do you read other people's opinions?

Crack the code

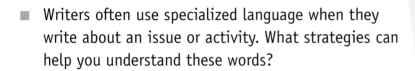

- Writers often use specialized language when they write about an issue or activity. What strategies can help you understand these words?

documentary
sitcom
docudrama
soap opera

Make meaning

Practise using these strategies when you read opinions:

USE WHAT YOU KNOW Before you read, look at the title and visuals to identify the topic. Then ask yourself: What do I already know about this topic?

VISUALIZE Use the details to imagine the event or situation.

SYNTHESIZE Put ideas together. How do the opinions and information compare with what you already know or believe?

Analyze what you read

- Think about who is writing or speaking. What do they want you to think or do? Why should you believe them?

- Who might disagree? Compare their ideas on the same topic.

Celebrities Good Role Models?

ACTOR RICK SLICK CHARGED

with speeding in his corvette...again!

NATIONAL CONSPIRATOR

Volume 1, Issue 3 2007

"He's had hair replacement, Botox treatments, and a chin tuck."

-Melissa Bouffant, hairstylist and long-time confidant

MEGA-STAR'S SECRETS REVEALED!

Darren Crick's Hairstylist Tells All!

Doctor Tells **Model Michelle:** "Eat More!"

superstar **Bratney** CAUGHT lip-synching *at concert!*

Hockey star paid **$1.5M** to appear in commercial

For display only

9 780132 053396

No Way!

by Elizabeth Harlow

I think celebrities are not good role models for young people. Some sports stars are too violent, super models look unrealistically thin, and celebrities push products that are not necessarily good for you. These are not good examples for kids.

Take this situation: a national hockey game. Fans from all over the country are there to watch. All of a sudden, a player throws off his gloves and attacks an opponent. Adult fans cheer the fighting. Small children who admire the hockey player are led to think that hockey is all about fighting to win. Next time those children play hockey, they may start fights themselves.

Think hard: Are celebrities really good examples to follow?

Now think about a young girl watching a fashion show on TV. On the catwalk, a very thin-waisted model, with a one-of-a-kind body shape, walks out in expensive clothing. The girl really wants to look like the model. She begins dieting and spending her money on fashionable clothes, in sizes way too small for her. She continues to diet, trying to fit into the expensive clothes. This is not healthy in any way. Very few people will ever look like that supermodel.

What about celebrity endorsements? When a celebrity advertises a soft drink or make-up, fans will want to buy that product even if it costs a lot and their parents don't approve. Some will do anything to get their hands on the product. Do parents want their kids to listen to the celebrity or to them?

So before you try to be like your favourite sports star, model, actor, or other celebrity, think hard. Is that person really a good example to follow?

VISUALIZE

Imagine acting like your favourite celebrity.

SYNTHESIZE

Compare your own opinions with those of the author.

Movie Ratings:

What Everyone Should Know About the Movie Rating System

GENERAL AUDIENCES

Open to all audiences. Nothing that would offend parents for viewing by children.

PARENTAL GUIDANCE SUGGESTED

May contain some material parents might not like for their young children.

PARENTAL ACCOMPANIMENT REQUIRED

Parents must accompany their children. Some material may be inappropriate for pre-teenagers or teenagers.

RESTRICTED

Contains adult material. Admittance is restricted to people 18 years of age or older.

Definitely!

by Luke Sengupta-Murray

Movie ratings are important. Know them!

Movie ratings are important because they help protect kids from watching movies with violence and mature content. If there were no movie ratings, young kids could just walk into a movie theatre and watch a horror movie. The experience could traumatize them for weeks! Movie ratings let kids know if a movie is okay for them to watch or not.

Some people think that age does not indicate maturity. They argue that some 12-year-olds are mature enough to watch movies with some violence, for example. That may be true, but it would be too hard for ticket-booth workers to ask questions that test maturity. Like it or not, age is the best measure of maturity that we have.

Other people suggest that kids already have too many rules. They claim that kids, like adults, should be free to make their own decisions and watch what they want. However, I disagree. Kids should not be allowed to watch movies with mature content because they are simply not ready. Kids need to be protected from some mature themes in movies because they may be negatively influenced by the content. The movie could upset them or encourage them to behave in inappropriate ways.

Movie ratings are guidelines to follow. They help kids judge what is appropriate and help them decide if they are mature enough to watch a particular movie. So the next time you are not allowed into a restricted movie, before you get upset, think about what could happen if you *did* watch the movie!

VISUALIZE
Imagine what it would be like if there were no movie ratings.

SYNTHESIZE
Compare your own opinions with those of the author.

13

Movie Ratings:

DALT WISNEY'S
—PICTURES—
Presents

DINO-SOAR

G
GENERAL AUDIENCES

USE WHAT YOU KNOW

What do you already know about movie ratings?

FIRST 100 ticket buyers receive a free Dino-Soar action figure*
BUY YOUR TICKETS TODAY !

Action figures valued at $19.99/each.

14

No Thanks!

by Jeffrey Probert

Do you agree with government ratings on movies? I am against ratings that prevent people from watching what they enjoy. I think parents should decide what their kids can watch, *not* the government.

Parents and guardians are the ones who are with kids in the home. They have raised their kids and know them best. If a young child is watching a movie that is not appropriate, then the parents or guardians must deal with the situation. They need to closely monitor what their child watches—not just rely on what the government says.

Not all families have the same ideas about what is appropriate. For instance, a movie could be rated for general audiences because it doesn't have a lot of violence. But it may be inappropriate in some other way. Perhaps it was made just to advertise a certain action figure that is animated in the movie. Watching the movie might encourage kids to want to buy the toy. Some parents or guardians might not agree with this, so in their minds the movie is not appropriate. If they rely on the rating system, their kids will be influenced in a way they don't want.

Or, let's say a movie is rated as having some violence. Parents or guardians may believe the movie has a good message for their kids. They may feel that their kids are mature enough to handle the content and won't be negatively influenced.

How can the government really know or monitor kids? The government can't come into their homes every day. Parents and guardians are better able to guide their kids and talk to them about why some movies are not appropriate for them to watch.

So, I think the government should do away with ratings. Let parents and guardians decide!

Take a look at the poster. Is it a G-rated movie or an advertisement for an action figure? Why even rate it?

VISUALIZE
Imagine what it would be like if there were no movie ratings.

SYNTHESIZE
Compare your own opinions with those of the author.

15

Reflect on Your Reading

You have . . .

- talked about entertainment students enjoy.
- read other students' opinions about celebrity role models and movie ratings.
- used strategies to read challenging words.

celebrities

maturity

traumatize

guidelines

inappropriate

I like listening to alternative rock. What about you?

USE WHAT YOU KNOW

VISUALIZE

SYNTHESIZE

You have also . . .

- explored different reading strategies.

Write About Learning

How does comparing your own opinions to a writer's opinions help you think about what you read? Write about how this strategy helps you.

Read Like a Writer

You can learn how to write convincing opinions by analyzing what other writers do. How do they develop their arguments and reasons? How do they persuade people to agree with their ideas?

TALK ABOUT IT!

- What do you notice about the kinds of information in opinion articles?

- How does the writer make you stop and think?

- What makes the ideas convincing?

HINT!

Look at the **reasons** the writers use to support their opinions.

Ideas in Opinion Writing

- the opinion is stated clearly at the beginning
- the writer gives examples that the reader will understand
- the writer includes the most convincing reasons
- the conclusion strongly restates the writer's opinion

17

WHAT'S THE

by Jessica Westhead
Illustrated by Dave Whamond

Why do people watch reality TV?

REALITY?

Imagine this: You sit down to dinner and ask your dad to please pass the salt and pepper. Instead of handing you the black and white shakers, he grabs a microphone and starts singing about them. He takes a bow and your brother says, "That was the worst salt-and-pepper song I've ever heard. You're fired!"

Then your mom asks if you're ready for the main course. But it's not your real mom—it's a mom from somebody else's family! She puts a steaming plate in front of you and says, "I hope you like my worm-and-maggot stew!"

"You'd better eat it," says your sister. "That's all we could find in the jungle, and we need the energy for tomorrow's challenges. You don't want to get kicked off the island, do you?"

"Okay," you say, and pick up your fork. You look right into one of the cameras, and take a big bite.

This is just a **TASTE** of some of the reality shows that have been on TV. Reality TV is television programming that shines the spotlight on ordinary people in extraordinary situations. You can find reality shows on almost every channel. Opinions about this television trend are divided—viewers seem to either love it or hate it. Keep reading to find out why.

READ LIKE A WRITER

How does the writer balance pros and cons for the reader?

REALITY TV: HOT...

Why do some people think reality TV shows are worth watching?

N-N-NICE SNAKE!

Overcoming your fears

Reality shows can help people overcome their fears. Maybe performing in front of an audience is what scares you most—or maybe it's eating a plateful of worm-and-maggot stew. Whatever you're afraid of, it's inspiring to see somebody just like yourself facing a similar fear, and beating it.

Real people, real possibilities

Instead of featuring too-perfect celebrities who grab so much of our attention nowadays, reality TV focuses on real people. Viewers get a glimpse into real people's lives, not just the lives of characters acting out a fictional storyline. They also see "regular folks" going after their dreams—and tackling obstacles along the way. This gives young viewers something real to aspire to, rather than an unreal, Hollywood-type existence.

Fun for the whole family

Reality shows are entertaining to watch with other people. Getting caught up in the action is fun—and it's even better when friends and family members are cheering or booing with you. Many reality programs also promote teamwork. They offer examples of people from different backgrounds looking past their differences to reach a common goal.

OR NOT?

So what's the problem with reality TV?

Don't try this at home!

A lot of reality TV programs show people doing unsafe and even dangerous things. There have been reports of children, and sometimes adults, injuring themselves by trying to act out what they have seen on TV. People often don't realize that these shows use safety equipment and trained professionals on set.

How "real" is this reality?

Kids who watch a lot of reality shows that promote wealth or fame as the only worthy achievements can come away with unreasonable expectations for their own lives. Not "measuring up" can lead to feelings of dissatisfaction. The "reality" depicted on reality shows can discourage kids from living in the present and taking pride in their own accomplishments.

The best of the worst?

Reality TV isn't real—it's a producer's *version* of reality. Episodes are edited to show the most exciting bits and may feature people at their nastiest. Some experts think that reality TV highlights the worst parts of human nature and can encourage viewers to copy the inappropriate behaviour they see onscreen.

WHAT'S YOUR OPINION?

Now it's time to decide for yourself! Are reality shows harmless, inspirational entertainment…or TV that's hazardous to your health?

Reality TV—Good Clean Fun or Bad Influence?

PROS	CONS
• Helps people conquer their fears	• Can encourage viewers to copy dangerous stunts
• Offers empowering examples of real people living real lives	• Promotes unrealistic expectations that can be harmful to people's self-image
• Fosters teamwork	• Rewards inappropriate behaviour

MEDIA WATCH

Collect articles and reviews that discuss reality TV shows. What positive and negative effects do they suggest?

DIG DEEPER

1. Which is more convincing to you—the pro or con arguments? Make an outline for a letter to a TV station giving your opinion about reality shows.

2. Think about a reality show you know about. Redesign it to avoid the "cons" in this article.

What Type of Gamer Are You?

by Clive Thompson

READ LIKE A WRITER

How does the writer use his own experiences to make the issue clear?

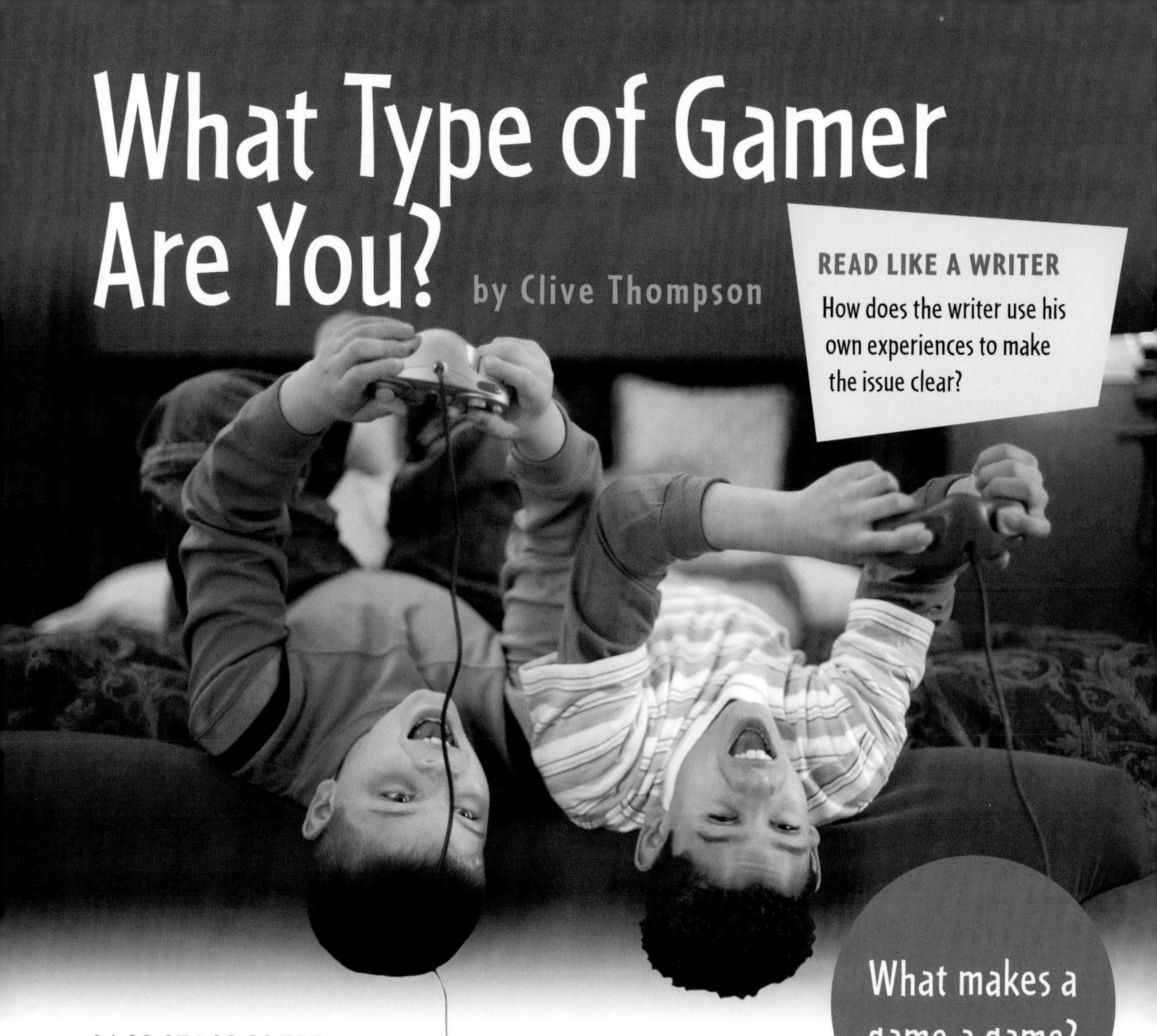

What makes a game a game?

04.23.07 | 02:00 PM

A month ago while playing an online multiplayer game, I fought my way to a huge, clawed dragon—and couldn't get past it. No matter how many ways I threw my team at the beast, it turned us back. I decided to check an online FAQ for some hints.

"That's cheating," a friend of mine scoffed. "Really?" I wondered. Personally, I've always figured that using a FAQ might be lame, but I never thought it was cheating.

We never agreed, but our argument reminded me of something quite interesting: Video game players often hold very different views on what constitutes "cheating."

FAQ

frequently asked question(s)

23

It didn't used to be as hard to figure out. In traditional games, cheating was—and still is—usually obvious. Slathering a baseball in spit or moving chess pieces when your opponent goes to the bathroom—yeah, that's cheating.

Today's multiplayer games are different from the old-school stuff. If players use **walkthroughs**, such as progressive hints, to guide them to the solution, many gamers think it's a form of cheating. But where things get weird is with single-player video games.

What exactly are the "rules" in a single-player game, anyway? You're not competing against another human. You're battling the computer and, in a sense, yourself. On top of that, the game producers actually hide secret **power-ups** inside the games. They also work together on the creation of walkthroughs and game guides.

Mia Consalvo, a professor at Ohio University, interviewed dozens of players about their attitudes and found that we cluster into a couple of groups.

A small group is considered die-hard purists, like my friend. They don't use any "cheats" or guides because they consider it "cheating yourself" of the subtle pleasure of getting stuck in a game—then suddenly spying the way out.

The next group is the walkthrough folks, like me. We regard guides as a form of travel literature. I would have never located all the cool, secret areas in that multiplayer game without a FAQ. I almost never use help tactics to grant myself "unearned" power.

Then there's the final group of gamers—the "by any means necessary" crowd. In their view, cheating in a single-player game isn't possible. As one interviewee told Consalvo, "You can't cheat a game system—you can only cheat another player." For example, if part of the goal in a narrative game is to finish the story, what's wrong with using any tool at hand to do so?

I personally disagree with the "by any means necessary" position. I think self-imposed limits are what make a game a *game*. What do you think?

walkthrough

a document that attempts to teach a player how to beat or solve a particular game

power-up

an item in a game that gives the player added powers when it's touched or collected

24

Comments

Well, if those walkthroughs are on the Internet, then I don't see any harm in actually using them for those tough spots you can't get through. But if you use them for every little thing, then that's what I would call cheating.

Posted by: Topthat4

I don't like to use walkthroughs. I like to beat any game once on the hard level through my own skill before using any outside assistance—other than a few tips from friends here and there. Otherwise, it just seems like I'm cheating myself out of knowing that I did the whole game by myself.

Posted by: Skilldog

DIG DEEPER

1. Use the information in this article to make a chart comparing the views of the three groups the author describes. Which group best matches your opinion?

2. Respond to this blog by writing your own comment. Then exchange with at least two other students, and write responses to each other's comments.

Entertainment

What amazing facts can you learn about arts and entertainment?

The Beatles have sold more records than anyone else with over a billion worldwide.

In **Jurassic Park**, the roar of the T. Rex came from mixing the sounds of a crocodile, a lion, a tiger, and a baby elephant.

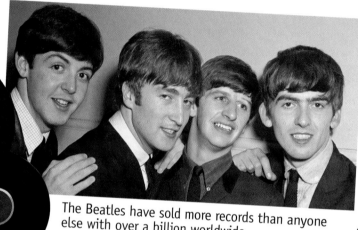

In 1938, Joe Shuster and Jerry Siegel sold all rights to the comic-strip character Superman to their publishers for $130.

The ruby red slippers in the movie **The Wizard of Oz** were sold off at an auction for $660 000.

Trivia

READ LIKE A WRITER
How does the writer use specific details to make the trivia interesting?

Famous comedian Charlie Chaplin once entered a Charlie Chaplin look-alike contest. He didn't even make the finals!

Singer Céline Dion became so famous that a 4000-seat arena was built for her to perform in Las Vegas. Quite a rise to fame for this youngest of 14 siblings from a small Quebec town!

It took four people to play Darth Vader in **Star Wars**. David Prowse was his body. James Earl Jones did his voice. Sebastian Shaw was his unmasked face, and a fourth person did his breathing.

The characters of Homer, Marge, Lisa, and Maggie have the same first names as the real-life father, mother, and two sisters of **The Simpsons'** creator, Matt Groening.

27

The costume designer for Disney's **Pirates of the Caribbean** put the pirate costumes through a cement mixer. They were frayed and overdried to create a dirty and unwashed look.

What's the movie capital of the world? No, it's not Hollywood. It's Bollywood! This nickname comes from combining the word *Hollywood* with *Bombay*, the former name of the city of Mumbai, in India. Mumbai produces about twice as many films annually as the United States!

DIG DEEPER

1. With a partner, choose one of the trivia items. Create a short role play or interview where you ask and answer questions about the interesting fact or accomplishment.

2. Research to find your own entertainment trivia or "believe it or not" fact. Illustrate your fact and share it with the class.

Artistic Expressions

by Edward O'Connor

READ LIKE A WRITER

How does the writer use unusual information to create interest?

What do you think of when you hear the word *artist*? Many people imagine someone painting a picture. Actually, there are many different kinds of artists, and many different ways to express yourself through art. Check out the Canadian artists shown here. Then decide what form of art *you* would choose to express yourself.

What different artforms do people use to express themselves?

Joseph Wu, Origami Artist

Origami is the ancient Japanese art of paper folding. Joseph Wu has been practising this art since he was three years old. He can fold a piece of paper to make it look like just about anything from sharks and dragons to cell phones and computers. He likes to create fantasy figures as well, such as characters from graphic novels and video games.

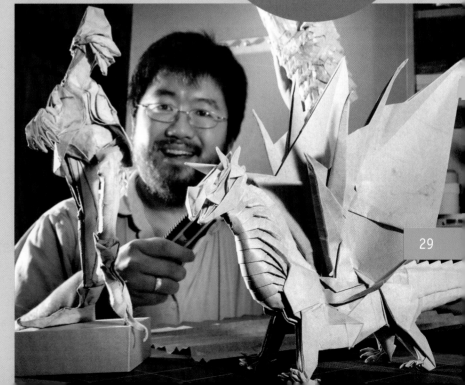

29

Junkyard Symphony

Most symphony orchestras play classical music on expensive instruments, such as violins and trumpets. Junkyard Symphony is different. This group of musicians uses recycled junk to make rock music and perform magic and juggling shows. If you ever go to see them, you may wind up on stage yourself. The group leader, Johnny Junkyard, will show you how to juggle or drum, or even do the limbo. Junkyard Symphony has an important message to spread: Reduce, reuse, recycle, and ROCK!

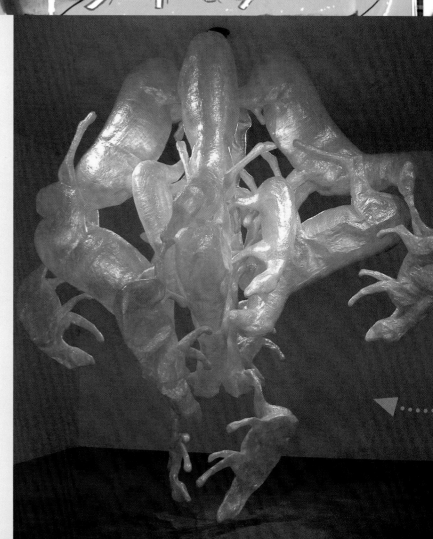

David Hannan, Sculptor

David Hannan is a Métis artist from Ottawa. This sculpture is one of many David has created using animal forms. It has coyote and deer shapes made out of clear packing tape! The figures are hung from the ceiling like a huge chandelier. When the light shines through the transparent tape, it creates a beautiful and mysterious glow. David says his culture is reflected in his artwork. The coyote, for example, is a common trickster figure in many Aboriginal stories. David created this sculpture so that people would ask questions about the relationship between humans and animals.

Théâtre Sans Fil

Imagine giant, life-sized puppets on stage. Théâtre Sans Fil, or Theatre Without Strings, is a unique group of puppeteers. Their style is based on an ancient Japanese method called *Bunraku*. Several puppeteers, dressed in black, operate each of the colourful, life-sized puppets. Although the audience can see the puppeteers, their attention is fully drawn to the colourful puppets themselves.

Maud Lewis, Folk Artist (1903-1970)

Maud Lewis is Nova Scotia's most famous folk artist. Maud never had much money, but she loved to paint. She painted every surface in the tiny house she lived in with her husband, Everett. The wallpaper, door, kitchen cabinets, and even the dustpan and stove of the house were painted with farm animals, butterflies, birds, and flowers. Now her whole house stands in the Art Gallery of Nova Scotia.

Alan Shain, Comedian

A comedian is an artist whose skill is making people laugh. Alan Shain has cerebral palsy (CP), a condition that makes it hard for him to control his movements. He uses comedy to help people understand his life better. Alan jokes that, because his electric wheelchair weighs 91 kg, his favourite game in school was tug-of-war! He has performed on stages across North America and Australia and often gives comedy workshops in schools.

Phyllis Grant, Multidisciplinary Artist

Hip hop artist. Illustrator. Animator. Poet. Photographer. Phyllis Grant just doesn't seem to know how *not* to be creative. This young Mi'kmaw woman from New Brunswick has been nominated for an East Coast Music Award for her songwriting. She has exhibited her artwork in Canada and abroad. If that's not enough, she's also written, drawn, and directed an animated film produced by the National Film Board of Canada. Oh, and she's writing a book of poetry. Being called an artist doesn't necessarily mean being good at just one thing. Many artists have several "gifts" and are multi-talented like Phyllis Grant!

DIG DEEPER

1. Which artist do you find most interesting? What questions would you ask if you could interview this person? Share your ideas with a partner or small group.

2. Choose another artist you know about and whose work you enjoy. Using this selection as a model, write a short profile on that artist.

Publishers at Work!

You have read and viewed articles about arts and entertainment. Now it's your turn to make your own entertainment magazine.

Plan Your Magazine

- Work in a group. Choose a topic in arts and entertainment that is important to you.

- You might choose a type of music, a style of art, or a different form of entertainment, such as video games. Or you could choose to focus on your favourite group or artist.

- Assign each person in your group to write one opinion article. It can be a review, an editorial, a blog, one or more letters to the editor, or any other form of opinion you choose. It might even be a comic strip!

Write Your Article

- Think about your purpose: What do you want your readers to learn, think, or do?

- Look back at examples of opinion pieces you read in this unit. Collect reviews, letters to the editor, and other opinion articles from other magazines.

- Use a graphic organizer to plan your article.

- Write a draft. Revise it with a partner or group.

- Remember: Be persuasive and convincing!

Publish Your Magazine

- Use a computer to produce your finished articles.

- Collect the articles. Then work together to create a cover and other features for your magazine, such as ads, pictures, table of contents, etc.

- Publish it! Place your finished magazines in your school or classroom library for other students to enjoy.

PRESENTATION POINTERS

- Use interesting lettering to catch the readers' attention.

- Leave lots of space between articles and in the margins.

- Use colour to help readers see what is most important on a page.

2

SPEAK OUT!

Goodwill Ambassadors: Do They Serve a Purpose?
by Addy Levine

Some people wonder why the UN and other good causes have celebrity ambassadors. Are they mostly performers who are only doing good deeds to try to save their dead careers? I think a few might do it for that reason, but not most of them.

The same way a flashy ad gets lots of attention for a new product and makes people buy it, seeing a popular star talking about an issue makes people pay attention and maybe even give money to the cause. When I see stories about Leo DiCaprio fighting for the environment, or Angelie Jolie doing work for the UN, I pay much more attention than I do to regular news stories. And many people who never read a newspaper or watch the news on TV often read celebrity magazines or look at celebrity Web sites. Maybe that's wrong, but that's the way it is. And when I asked my friends, they said the same thing.

In my opinion, so what if the celebrity gets some free publicity? In most cases, they could be doing work that would make them a lot of money. Instead, they spend their time travelling to places most of us wouldn't want to ever go. The attention they bring to world issues is worth more than the little bit of free publicity they get for their good deeds!

In My View

Celebrities Should Do More Than Just Talk
by Michel Ferrier

Last weekend I saw a movie with John Travolta in it. I liked the movie, so when I saw an article in the paper the next day with his picture, I picked it up. It wasn't an article about his movie, though, but about how he campaigns for saving the environment. But then the article talked about how he has several airplanes, and sometimes flies them when he's almost the only person on them. I got thinking about all the gas he's using, and all the pollution he's putting in the air. So now I wonder how many other people talk about a cause but don't really do anything serious in their own life to help.

It reminded me of the last world soccer tournament. Everyone talked about stopping racism and shook hands and agreed to change—but then some players said and did racist things right away during the games anyway.

It's good to talk about problems and try to come up with solutions. But I think people who are going to talk about supporting a cause need to do MORE than just talk.

Wristbands like these with "STAND UP/ SPEAK UP" on them were worn to protest racism in soccer.

3

Celebrities to the Rescue(?)
by Elliot Harmon and Cara Chayter

June 1
Famous celebrity agent Del De Sousa phones some young actors to offer them great publicity.

July 5
The actors arrive for the photo shoot that's supposed to show their support for saving the Earth…

Sept. 15 TOO LATE!

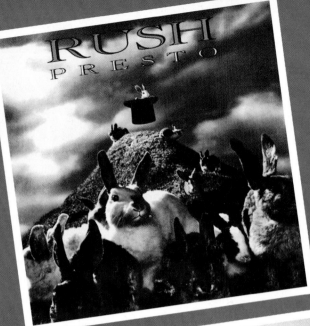

What does a CD cover tell you about the artist?

Design

THE DUHKS
MIGRATIONS

Eagle & Hawk

mother earth

Explosion!

bryan adams: on a day like today

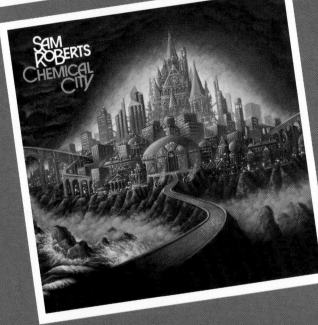

DIG DEEPER ·····················

1. Make a table summarizing the images, titles, artists, and main impressions conveyed by the CD covers.

Image	Title	Artist	Main Impression

2. Choose one of your favourite groups or artists. Design a CD cover for their next release.

37

Learn a Dance Move!

by Mandy Ng

Illustrated by Tina Holdcroft

HOW CAN YOU WRITE DOWN A DANCE MOVE?

STEP 1

Hop on your left foot as you **KICK** your right foot to the front. At the same time, throw both arms in front of your body.

STEP 2

STEP your right foot over your left foot and cross your arms in front of your chest.

STEP 3

TOUCH your left foot to the side while you snap your arms down to the sides of your body in the shape of an "A."

Learn the Kick-Step-Touch:

an off-the-hook hip hop move that will get a dance party started!

You'll need:

- comfortable clothes
- tied shoes
- hip hop music

READ LIKE A WRITER

How does the writer use specific details to make the moves easy to understand?

STEP 4

Now take your moves to the other side! Hop on your right foot and **KICK** your left foot to the front. Throw both arms in front of your body.

STEP 5

STEP your left foot over your right foot and fold your arms.

STEP 6

TOUCH your right foot to the side and pop your arms down to the sides of your body. Groove back to Step 1 and start again!

DIG DEEPER

1. Practise the move with a partner. Help each other by taking turns reading the instructions and giving feedback. If you can, put your moves to music.

2. With a partner, invent a new dance move and write the instructions. Trade the instructions with another pair to try out the dance move.

39

Perfect

How can you "see" sounds?

RhyThm Is

Drumsticks tick
tick tick tick
rhythmic licks
with a flick
of the wrist.
Like the thump
of a drum
rhythm hums
a track
for voices
to glide
slide and
ride
upon.
Creating constant
sound
with a background
beat,
rhythm is the
clock
that keeps
vocal cords
on their feet.
Setting lyrics
in motion,
rhythm is
an ocean
filled with
the

pump-pump
pump-pump

sound of
heartbeats
the

jump-jump
jump-jump

of double-Dutch
feet
keeping time
with rope
skip
skip
skipping on concrete
the dribble-dribble
stop
that makes
jumpshots
drop
the

pop-pop
pop-pop-pop

sound of kernels
getting hot.
From a nod
of the head

to a
  shake
shake
  shake
of
the feet
rhythm lives in you
rhythm lives in me
rhythm in the song
of life
breaks
breaks
down
to one
simple key:
marching your own
voice
to your own
rhythmic
beat.

READ LIKE A WRITER
How does the poet help
readers "hear" the
rhythms in the music?

Harmony

by Charles R. Smith, Jr.

ALTO HAiKU

Alto notes drift high
in the sky lingering
beneath soprano wings.

BASS HAiKU

Buried in the deep
reaches of the belly; bass
booms deep and heavy.

TENOR HAIKU

Not too heavy, not
too soft, tenor hits notes like
a velvet hammer.

MEDIA WATCH

Collect articles about musicians. Make a chart summarizing who the artists are, what kind of music is featured, and whether the articles are mostly positive or negative. Summarize what you notice.

SOPRANO HAIKU

Songbirds sing in
sweet soprano
voices; hitting
high notes easily.

DIG DEEPER

1. With a group, choose a way to present "Rhythm Is" including sounds to make it interesting and meaningful. Share your performance with other groups.

2. With a partner, create your own haiku about music or a musical instrument and illustrate it.

The Mona Lisa Caper

by Rick Jacobson

Illustrated by Laura Fernandez & Rick Jacobson

How can a painting come
to life and tell a story?

READ LIKE A WRITER

How does the writer use details to make Mona Lisa's voice seem real?

Hanging on a wall year after year is not as easy as you might think. In fact, it's tiring, and I often wish I could take a holiday. Once, very long ago, I did just that. Of course, I had quite a bit of help.

It was 1911, and the world-famous Louvre Museum in Paris was in an uproar. Many of its treasures, including me, were being photographed so that the museum staff could keep track of us all. At the same time, workers were hired to make display cases for many of the paintings. One of those workers became a friend of mine. His name was Vincenzo Perugia.

Vincenzo built the box that now held me safe. Every day at noon, he sat before me, eating his sandwich and speaking in Italian. At first I found it hard to understand him. You see, although I had been painted in Italy by the great genius, Leonardo da Vinci, I hadn't heard the language spoken for a long time. Little by little I began to understand everything he said. He talked about Italy and how homesick he was, and as he spoke, a strange feeling came over me. I realized that I missed my country too. I missed the fresh air and the smells and the people in the streets. Though I tried to tell Vincenzo, he couldn't hear me.

Then one day, with his mouth still full of his last bite, he said something that surprised me.

"I think you miss Italy as much as I."

After a short pause, Vincenzo went back to work.

Early in the morning a few days later, Vincenzo came and took me down from the wall. I was very excited. I was also frightened!

My friend wrapped me in a big cloth and tied it firmly. As luck would have it, there was a small hole near my right eye and I could see out.

Vincenzo carried me through galleries and down stairs. He ran into a little trouble when he came to a locked side door, but someone came along and taking no notice of me, helped as Vincenzo removed the doorknob.

Vincenzo slipped the doorknob into his pocket, thanked the man, and left the Louvre—just like that. It was the first time I had been outside in over a hundred years. It was wonderful!

Up until now, I had never really seen the city. Paris was beautiful, especially in the morning light as the sun rose higher and cast a warm glow over everything. Vincenzo walked quickly, pausing only to toss the doorknob from his pocket as we wound through twisting alleys toward his home.

It was wonderful!

He lived in a small third-floor flat. Each morning before Vincenzo headed off to work, he would slip me under his bed and I would simply listen. When he returned, he would bring me out, remove my cloth, and set me on a chair a short distance from a window. I could see the Paris skyline with its twinkling lights and hear outside noises. Vincenzo would talk about everything—his home in Italy and his work.

And so it continued. During the day, I remained under the bed and listened to everyone who lived in and around the building. I grew to know shopkeepers, bankers, mothers, and children by their voices. At night from my chair, I enjoyed Vincenzo's stories and the magic of Paris nights. I couldn't imagine being happier, but then, I didn't know what was in store for me.

At first Vincenzo was nervous. He told me the museum was crawling with gendarmes and inspectors, all looking for me. He was afraid they would discover that he was the one who had taken me from the Louvre. In fact, they did question him, but they let him go. He read me newspaper stories about the kidnapping, and he told me what he had heard about the investigation.

I listened to the talk on the street. People were very upset. They missed me and I felt guilty for enjoying my freedom. If only I could tell Vincenzo, but my lips were painted firmly in place. They smiled, but would not form words.

One morning Vincenzo did not go to work. He went out and didn't return until dusk. He took me out from under the bed, but did not unwrap me or put me on my chair. Instead, he set me by the door, muttering that it was time for us to leave. Someone had found the doorknob. The French police were asking too many questions. Vincenzo and I were going to escape to our homeland!

When Vincenzo was ready, he picked me up and headed for the street. It was late October and it was raining—not hard, but I could feel it in the air. Vincenzo tenderly placed me on the back seat of his little car and drove away. As we left, I thought about the neighbours I would never see or hear again.

The ride through Paris was long and the noises and smells kept changing. Vincenzo seemed tense and pushed the little car through traffic, often blasting the horn, only to be answered by other horns. I was happy when the city sounds were eventually replaced by the *pssssh* of our tires on wet country roads.

The French police were asking too many questions.

Gradually Vincenzo relaxed and began to talk to me. At first he spoke only about what we were passing, but as his tension eased, he described Italy for me. No vehicles had passed us for some time when Vincenzo slowed the car. The sound of the tires changed as they left the pavement, crunched on gravel, then stopped on a deserted side road. Vincenzo turned the engine off, shifted in his seat, and within minutes I heard his familiar deep breathing. He was asleep.

Hour after hour I listened to the night noises of small creatures. Their quiet rustlings gradually gave way to a chorus of birdsong as the sun rose.

Vincenzo woke with a big stretch, and within minutes we were on our way again. The road was dry today and the little car seemed livelier. Vincenzo burst into song. Still covered on the back seat, I listened. The traffic was light and the road, although curvy, was smooth. The sun shone through the window and warmed me in a faintly familiar way. It was delicious.

Vincenzo rolled down the window and I could smell the sweet scent of grass, wet with morning dew. Cuckoos called over the purr of the car's engine. A playful gust of wind loosened my wrapping and suddenly I could see. My eyes filled with the warm yellow light of a glorious day. We rushed past trees and I recognized them. They mirrored the ones painted behind me. I was back in the land where I had been created! It was beautiful—so full of colour, sound, and fragrance. Those precious few hours on that road were the happiest in all my five hundred years.

By early evening, Florence lay before us. We had come over a low hill and Vincenzo announced, "We're home."

He reached behind and pulled my covering back into place. I was able to catch only a quick glimpse of the magnificent dome and marble towers at the city's centre, the criss-cross of bridges, and the ribbon of river, shimmering gold in the sunset. Still, I recognized everything. This could only be Florence.

Vincenzo rented a small room at the Hotel Tripoli, and just as in Paris, the window opened onto the world I had missed for many years.

We settled into our familiar routine. Every day I listened under the bed and every evening I watched Florence from my window. We were happy for several months. Then one evening I heard unfamiliar voices in our room.

Vincenzo and I were not alone!

Vincenzo and I were not alone!

I was brought out from under the bed and my wrapping was removed. Two strangers stood before me with shocked expressions on their faces. One leaned forward and peered at me for a closer look. I soon learned that he was an art dealer named Alfredo Geri. His friend was Giovanne Poggie. I didn't like them, and I certainly didn't trust them.

Vincenzo rambled on about Italy and the rights of the people and many other things I didn't really understand. As the two men examined me, they exchanged secret glances. Something was terribly wrong and Vincenzo didn't seem to notice. I tried to warn him, to catch his attention, but once more, my words were sealed in the paint and Vincenzo couldn't hear me.

And then, to my horror, I realized that Vincenzo had sold me! Alfredo tied my covering around me, but just before I was wrapped in darkness, my eyes met Vincenzo's. There was the deep sadness of goodbye in them. Without words, I said goodbye too. Our great adventure was over. I never saw Vincenzo again.

I never saw Vincenzo again.

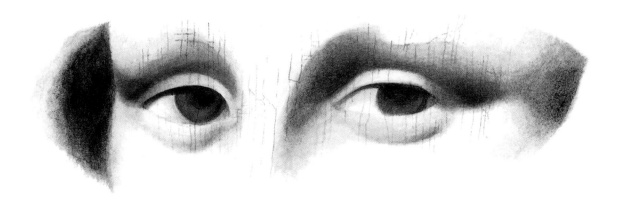

Once more, I was taken through the streets of Florence, but there was no enjoyment this time. I could only wonder what Vincenzo would do; where he would go now. When my cover was finally lifted, I was back in the still air of a museum. Again, people seemed surprised to see me. They examined me, compared me to photographs, scrutinized my brush strokes, and even inspected the cracks in my varnish. With great satisfaction they wisely concluded I was who I had been all along—Leonardo da Vinci's Mona Lisa.

A uniformed detective arrived and spoke with Alfredo and Giovanne. They told him how they had bought me and called the authorities, realizing I was the painting everyone was looking for. And they talked about my friend. When the detective left, I knew Vincenzo was in serious trouble.

Before my return to the Louvre I toured Italy, visiting museums in Florence, Milan, and Rome. I didn't mind being back. Not really. People were so happy to see me and more than once I overheard them talking about Vincenzo. He had been arrested, of course, and put on trial. After that he was released. I thought he might come to see me, but I suppose that he could not.

If *you* ever come to visit and notice me smiling my own private little smile, you will know it's because I'm lost in pleasant thoughts, remembering a holiday—remembering a friend.

Leonardo da Vinci painted the *Mona Lisa* between 1503 and 1506. Although it is not shown to scale for this story, the actual portrait is quite small— 53 cm × 77 cm—and was painted in oils on a poplar wood panel. For five hundred years, people have been fascinated by the lady with the smile. In Italy she is called *La Gioconda*. In France she is known as *La Joconde*. Both terms mean "the lighthearted woman" and they refer to the name of the lady who sat for the picture. Lisa Gherardini Giocondo would likely have smiled more broadly had she known how many people would eventually come to see her face and how widely travelled her portrait would be.

DIG DEEPER

1. Draw an illustrated map to represent the events in this story in the order they happened.

2. Make a chart showing Vincenzo's positive and negative actions in this story. Then write a short statement you would make to the judge about whether or not Vincenzo should have gone to jail.

Athena and Arachne

by Cirro Oh
Illustrated by C.S. Chun

READ LIKE A WRITER
How does the artist use details to emphasize the personality of each character?

Athena was one of the most powerful of the ancient Greek gods. She was the goddess of wisdom and justice. She also introduced weaving and other crafts to the people of Greece.

One day, Athena and Poseidon, the god of the sea, held a contest to see who would control the largest city in Greece. They agreed to give a gift to the people and let the citizens decide which gift was best. Poseidon gave the gift of water, but it was too salty to drink. Athena presented the people with an olive tree, which provided them with food, oil, and wood. From then on, the city was named Athens after its new patron goddess.

How could artistic talent get someone in trouble?

Athena, who won the competition for the city, faced another contest with a maiden named Arachne.

Arachne was beautiful. She was also famous for her great talent for weaving.

When Arachne worked on a weaving, a crowd of people and even the nymphs of forests and fountains came to see her.

Isn't it amazing?

It would take us millions of years to do as well as that.

Where did she learn such skills?

53

Maybe Athena, the goddess of weaving, trained her!

Yeah, I bet you're right! The tapestry could only be that beautiful if Arachne was trained by the goddess.

What do you mean by that?

What made you think that Athena trained me? I did not learn from anyone!

W-well...we just thought that your skill is too great to be from a mortal...

You really didn't learn from the goddess?

Of course not! If you don't believe me, let Athena try her skill against mine.

I don't think it's possible, but if I'm beaten by her, I will pay the penalty.

Athena heard this and was very displeased.

How dare she! That arrogant woman!

If I let her keep insulting a god without being punished, I will lose the people's respect!

The goddess disguised herself as an old woman and went to visit Arachne.

Is this where a maiden named Arachne lives?

Yes, I'm Arachne. Why are you looking for me, old woman?

Oh, what an amazing skill you have!

Hahaha... That's very sweet of you. Thank you.

But my dear, let me give you some advice.

What advice?

Please take no offence. You see, I'm old enough to know what the world is like, so please listen to what I'm trying to say to you now.

I heard that you wanted to compete with a goddess. You can compete with any human, but you just don't say that you can compete with a goddess and win.

You might be punished by the goddess for saying such a thing. So, why don't you go to the temple of the goddess Athena and offer an apology? Then the gracious goddess would forgive you.

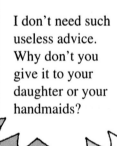

I don't need such useless advice. Why don't you give it to your daughter or your handmaids?

I will not take my words back no matter what happens.

I'm not at all afraid of the goddess Athena. Why doesn't she come down here to compete with me right now? Or is she scared?

Athena was enraged by Arachne's arrogance.

Very well, then here I come!

Athena dropped her disguise, and her body gave out a golden light and a sweet fragrance.

Ohhh...the goddess Athena's here!

Oh, goddess, I bow to you.

Pah.

They started their competition.

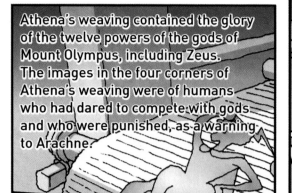

Athena's weaving contained the glory of the twelve powers of the gods of Mount Olympus, including Zeus. The images in the four corners of Athena's weaving were of humans who had dared to compete with gods and who were punished, as a warning to Arachne.

You are so arrogant! Take a close look at my weaving and give up this foolish contest, or you will be punished as well and you will regret what you have done forever.

What's so glorious about the gods? They make mistakes just as we do. Why are we forced to obey them? What nerve they have!

Disregarding Athena's warning, Arachne filled her weaving with images of the mistakes of the gods.

Finally, both finished their weaving.

Athena touched Arachne's forehead to make Arachne feel shame for her arrogance.

You rude girl! Now feel ashamed!

Where are you going?

Arachne? For your bad behaviour, you deserve the worst punishment, but I will let you remain on the Earth.

Arachne couldn't stand the embarrassment and she was in great despair. The goddess felt sorry for Arachne.

The goddess sprinkled Arachne with the sap from a plant.

You must weave forever. You will be here as a lesson for all future generations of what happens when a mortal dares to compete with the gods.

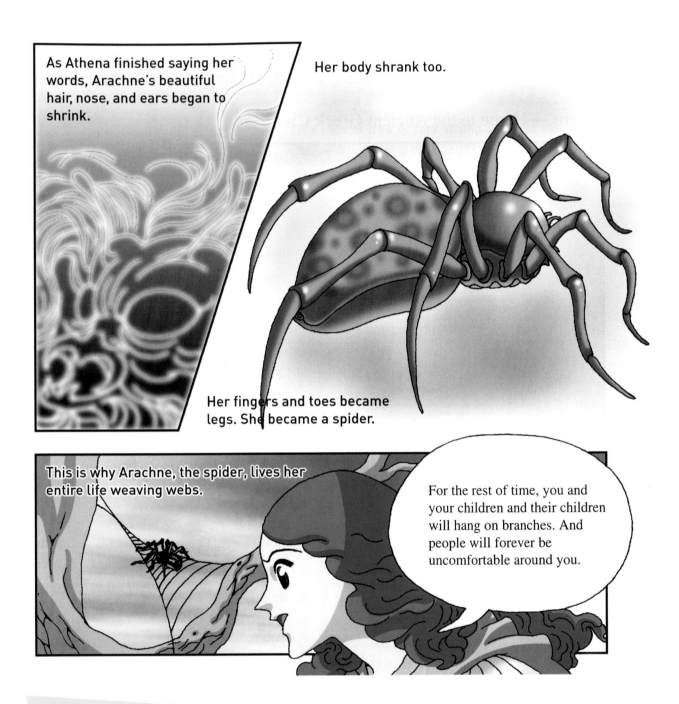

As Athena finished saying her words, Arachne's beautiful hair, nose, and ears began to shrink.

Her body shrank too.

Her fingers and toes became legs. She became a spider.

This is why Arachne, the spider, lives her entire life weaving webs.

For the rest of time, you and your children and their children will hang on branches. And people will forever be uncomfortable around you.

DIG DEEPER

1. Myths explain something important or teach a lesson about life. What important lesson or idea do you think this myth presented to ancient Greeks?

2. With a partner or small group, choose a myth from another culture (other than Greek or Roman) and recreate it as a graphic story.

61

Connect and Share

Everyone likes to talk about their favourite TV shows! Now it's your turn to share your opinion in a 30-second review!

Create your review!

- Choose a show you have a strong opinion about.
- Practise a powerful opening sentence that will hook your listeners' attention and clearly state your opinion.
- Give three reasons or examples to support your opinion.
- End by giving the show a rating, using one or two thumbs up or down.
- Your review should not take more than 30 seconds.

Share it with your family!

- Share your review with your family.
- Together, prepare another review of a show you all agree on.
- Use the same format.
- Bring your review back and share it with a group.

TIPS FOR PRESENTING

- Use facial expressions and gestures to emphasize your feelings about the show.
- Practise so your ideas come across clearly.
- Don't try to tell too much. Remember, 30 seconds isn't very long!

Spotlight on **Learning**

Collect

- Gather your notebooks, writing, and projects from this unit.

Talk and reflect

Work with a partner.

- Together, read the Learning Goals on page 2.
- Talk about how well you met these goals.
- Look over all your work for evidence.

Select

- Choose two pieces of work that you are most proud of that show your learning and how you achieved the Learning Goals. (The same piece of work can show more than one goal.)

Tell about your choices

- Tell why you chose each piece and how it shows your learning.

My choices	I want this in my portfolio because...

Reflect

- What have you learned about reading, viewing, listening to, and sharing opinions?
- What new information have you learned about arts and entertainment?

63

Stories
of Our Lives

LEARNING GOALS

In this unit you will

- Read, view, and listen to fictional stories that are realistic.

- Make inferences about characters and the points of view they present.

- Compare and connect stories in different forms and media.

- Create and present stories orally, in writing, and through media.

realistic fiction
character
plot
point of view
narrator
setting

How to Tell Tales

Illustrated by Dave Whamond

What are stories about?

1 Character vs. Nature

For example

Your sailing trip is hit by a freak storm, and you find yourself on a totally deserted island. Surviving on coconuts and a strange blue fruit that looks like an apple, you build a raft from tree branches and sail to safety. Fortunately, you pack some fruits—naming them "blues"—and on your return become a famous trader.

OR

You have been invited to an island for an advance tour of a new dinosaur theme park. Little do you know that the dinosaurs are real. A tropical storm approaches the island. Someone turns off the power and the T. Rex gets loose. You have to make it across the park to turn the power back on without getting chomped or stomped.

Stories twist and turn through our lives like snakes. As toddlers, we have them read to us; at the movies we watch them; and at school or at work we hear at least a dozen a day. But how do stories come about? The starting point is a conflict or problem of some kind. Many people believe that every story, no matter where it took place, when it happened, or by whom it was written, is based on one of these five basic conflicts.

2 Character vs. Character

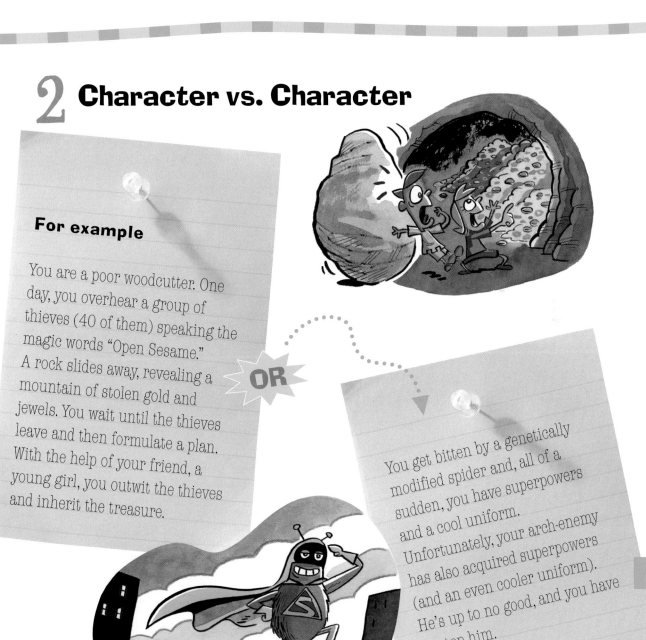

For example

You are a poor woodcutter. One day, you overhear a group of thieves (40 of them) speaking the magic words "Open Sesame." A rock slides away, revealing a mountain of stolen gold and jewels. You wait until the thieves leave and then formulate a plan. With the help of your friend, a young girl, you outwit the thieves and inherit the treasure.

OR

You get bitten by a genetically modified spider and, all of a sudden, you have superpowers and a cool uniform. Unfortunately, your arch-enemy has also acquired superpowers (and an even cooler uniform). He's up to no good, and you have to stop him.

3 Character vs. Society

OR

For example

You are an orphan with red hair and a strong imagination. An elderly brother and sister adopt you. You are grateful but you struggle to fit into their farming community. You often get into trouble, but eventually, the community comes to love you.

All you've ever wanted to do is draw cartoons, but everyone insists you take up a stable profession, such as teaching or banking. You endure brief social isolation, with only your drawings as comfort, but you eventually become a millionaire computer-game designer. Ha!

4 Character vs. Self

For example

It's the end of your birthday party. As you look around at the bobbing balloons and leftover cake, a voice in your head dejectedly shouts: "I wanted more people! I wanted more presents!" You then feel guilty for being so ungrateful. "I have it all," you think, "and I'm still not happy." Downer.

You are a wooden puppet with a nose that grows whenever you tell a lie. You desperately want to be a real human child. All you have to do is stay out of trouble, and your wish will be granted.

Unfortunately, you fall in with the wrong crowd, run away to the fair, and generally act like your own worst enemy. Eventually, though, you change your ways and start thinking of other people instead of yourself. Ping! Your wish is granted.

OR

5 Character vs. Machine

For example

Thanks to your new robotic rollerboots, you can do all the tricky moves you've been practising at the local park. A crowd flocks, and you do a fancy routine in time to music. Then suddenly you're flung from your skates and they speed away, twirling into the distance, leaving you feeling pretty foolish.

OR

Giant three-legged machines from outer space have taken over Earth. They have lasers for eyes. It's up to you to stop them. Good luck!

LET'S TALK ABOUT IT...

- Meet with a partner or group to share your ideas. Which of the examples reminded you of stories you know? Which kind of conflict do you usually like best? What other stories could you put in each of these categories?

- With your partner or group, create a basic plot for a story that would fit in one of these categories. Share your story with the class.

69

Reading Realistic Fiction

Many of the world's most popular stories are *realistic*—stories that could have happened, but didn't. These stories often have a narrator who is part of the plot. A narrator is the person who is telling the story. When we read, hear, or watch realistic stories, it's easy to imagine that we are there.

TALK ABOUT IT!

Think about realistic stories or novels you have read and realistic TV shows or movies you have seen.

- Who were the main characters?

- What were the stories about?

- Which stories were your favourites? Why?

Here are some places you can find realistic stories.

In a group, complete a chart like the one below.

Realistic Fiction	
Title	Description of one important character

Think Like a Reader

Read with a purpose

- Why might you read realistic fiction?

Crack the code

- Writers often use unusual expressions to catch their readers' interest. Sometimes the words don't mean exactly what they say. What "word picture" does this sentence paint? How would you explain, in everyday language, what the writer meant?

> "Stories twist and turn through our lives like snakes."

Make meaning

Practise using these strategies when you read fiction:

PREDICT — Look at the title and pictures. Think about what you already know about stories.

INFER — Read between the lines to figure out what the characters are thinking or feeling.

CONNECT — Think about how the story connects to other stories you have read or seen.

Analyze what you read

- Think about who is telling the story. How would the story be different if someone else told it?

- How does the story reveal the author's views about people?

Farzin's Story

Monday, June 10

Today I met a new friend. Well, he's not exactly new—but his personality certainly is. Let me explain.

Last week during Science class, I was trying to get a message to Eric to find out if he was available to play baseball that afternoon. He's not one to talk much but he's a good fielder, and we were going to need all the good players we could get.

Anyway, I used my usual method to get the message across the aisle to him. I scribbled the time and place on a piece of paper, crumpled it into a ball, and lobbed it. The only problem was the ball decided to sprout wings and fly over Eric's head. But as I said, Eric's a good fielder. He stretched his arm up really fast—just like one of those bullfrogs down by the creek flicks out its tongue to catch flies—and caught my note.

Suddenly, our teacher, Ms. Harab, was exclaiming, "Okay! There's our volunteer. Wonderful, Eric. Thank you!"

Eric?! Eric never volunteers for anything. He's really quiet and—unlike me—prefers never to be the centre of attention. Now, because of my lousy aim, he'd volunteered to represent our school at the district Peace Conference. Ouch!

For the next week, Eric didn't show up for baseball—not once. He looked worried, pale, nervous. I started to think he blamed me for getting him into such an impossible predicament, but when I tried to apologize, he didn't seem to want to discuss it. Of course, he never talks much, period. At least, the old Eric didn't.

The Peace Conference took place on Saturday. Today, he was back at school and, I swear, it was like he had been transformed into someone else. He actually put up his hand in class deliberately and answered a question—two, in fact—and out loud!

When I asked him about the Peace Conference, he didn't just shrug it off like the old familiar Eric might have. He told me all about it—all the way to the lunchroom, the whole time we were waiting in line, and even while we were sitting down eating our sandwiches. He didn't stop until we got up to take our trays to the counter. Then he asked if I wanted to join a new club he and Hilary were starting. The funny thing is, he was so inspiring, I think I will.

So there you go! Miracles can happen!

— Farzin

CONNECT

How does this story remind you of other stories you know?

Hilary's Story

PREDICT

What can you predict about the person who is telling the story?

Monday, June 10

I'm confused.

Last week, my teacher announced, "Hilary Lee will be our class representative at the district Peace Conference." I was thrilled! But then I met with Mr. Hay, our conference supervisor. That's when I discovered that Eric had volunteered to be the representative for the other class.

Don't get me wrong. Eric's a great guy—rock solid. But he's also about as talkative as…well, as a big mountain of rock! Since he came to our school last year, Eric's never volunteered to say or do anything.

Mr. Hay gave us materials to read and said things like, "This is a big opportunity for you both. You'll learn about peace issues around the world. You'll have an opportunity to express your points of view."

INFER

What is Eric likely thinking about Hilary?

No way. There was no way Eric would be saying anything in any of the sessions. And what was the point of him coming to a conference if he couldn't even participate in a discussion? I figured I would have to do all the talking.

I was so excited at the Peace Conference. I was on fast-forward all day, and I talked in almost every session. It was kind of cool that Eric was so quiet. It actually gave me more of an opportunity to share my opinions.

But then came the last session, and the strangest thing happened. Eric had been more and more agitated. He wasn't saying anything, but he was tapping his foot, tapping his pencil. And then, when the speaker was done and it was almost all over, Eric got up—and that mountain of rock *erupted!*

He spoke brilliantly. He was eloquent, charismatic, and persuasive. I was inspired!

And so today at first recess, when he asked me if I wanted to start a club with him, a club to get some social activism going, I actually said yes.

So there you go. Miracles can happen!

— Hilary

CONNECT

How does this story remind you of other stories you know?

Mr. Hay's Story

PREDICT

What can you predict about the person who is telling the story?

Monday, June 10

I'm ready to retire now. I've seen it all.

Last Saturday was the Peace Conference. For years, I've been our school's teacher representative and, every year, I've been pleased with the outcome. However, this year . . .

Well, it started badly. When I met with Hilary and Eric to discuss the conference, Eric didn't say a word. He wouldn't even look me in the eye. I was concerned, so I consulted his teacher, Ms. Harab.

"Eric's a puzzle," she explained. "He's very quiet, but he has lots of good ideas. And I must admit, he didn't actually volunteer for this," she added. "I picked him."

"No problem," I responded. However, I did wonder what might happen when a shy student was exposed to a roomful of outgoing and enthusiastic people who wanted to discuss important issues. Would he come out of his shell? Would he participate?

During the morning sessions, Hilary talked a lot, just as I expected she would. Eric looked almost relieved. I could tell he was absorbing it all, like a sponge, but he seemed as if he wasn't yet ready to communicate his ideas.

INFER

Why do you think Eric hardly ate?

As the hours passed, Eric appeared to become increasingly agitated. At lunchtime, he hardly ate anything. I got up to speak with him, but just then the bell rang, and we headed back to the auditorium.

Then the final session started. I can't remember the exact topic, but the speaker had concluded and was requesting comments and suggestions. Two students had responded briefly.

Then, shy, quiet Eric stood up—and he started speaking.

He hadn't raised his hand, and he hadn't been acknowledged. It was like some force was compelling him to get up and talk, almost against his will. Words poured out of him. Eric summarized the discussion and proposed a clear and concise plan of action. He spoke eloquently and passionately. By the time he finished, you could have heard a pin drop in the auditorium.

When Eric sat down, everyone burst into spontaneous applause, including Hilary and me, of course. My heart was doing somersaults inside my chest. I was so proud of Eric!

And so there you go. You just never know what might happen. Now I feel I've seen it all.

— Mr. Hay

CONNECT

How does this story remind you of other stories you know?

Reflect on Your Reading

You have . . .

- talked about reading and viewing realistic fiction.
- read stories about students your own age.
- explored words that are related to fiction.

realistic fiction

conflict

setting

character

narrator

dialogue

I like stories with a main character who changes or surprises me somehow.

PREDICT
INFER
CONNECT

You have also . . .

- explored three reading strategies.

Write About Learning

How do you figure out what a character is thinking and feeling? Write about how the inferences you make about the characters help you understand the stories you read.

Read Like a Writer

You can learn about the craft of writing fiction by analyzing what other writers do. Writers choose words or expressions that give each of their characters a unique "voice"—a way of speaking that brings out their personalities and points of view.

TALK ABOUT IT!

- How do writers make characters seem real and true-to-life?

- Why do writers often tell their stories through the eyes and words of one of the characters?

- List some of the ways writers create unique voices for their characters.

HINT!

Look at the way writers use **language** to tell you what the characters are like.

Giving Characters a "Voice"

- each character has his or her own way of speaking
- the way characters talk tells a lot about their personalities
- characters sound natural— they use everyday language
- if there is a narrator, he or she may also have a unique voice

A Blazing Rescue

by Donna Gamache   Illustrated by Leanne Franson

How can a cat be a hero?

One night in September, three days after my father had finished the harvesting, I was suddenly awakened by a loud meowing at my window. Somewhat startled, I quickly switched on my lamp and checked the time—it was just after midnight.

"What's up?" I mumbled, as I climbed out of bed and hurried to the window where my orange cat, Dandy—short for Dandelion— was still yowling. It was frosty that night, and I'd left the window open a bit—certainly not enough for her to crawl through it.

"Quiet, Dandy! You'll wake Dad." My father wasn't enthusiastic about cats. He didn't object to them in the barn to keep the mice under control, but he had no use for cats in the house. He hadn't an inkling that sometimes I smuggled Dandy into my room at night inside my shirt, or that frequently she climbed the tree outside my window, jumped onto the veranda roof, and climbed into my room.

I opened the window a bit more and stood back. "Come on in, Dandy, but keep it quiet."

My cat didn't move but continued to yowl.

"Come in!" I whispered with some impatience. "Or go back to the barn if you're cold."

I reached out to grab her, but she scooted out of my reach. Raising the window further, I leaned out, but she moved to the edge of the roof and meowed again—loudly. I just managed to see her in the light from the barnyard.

Light from the barnyard! I immediately scrambled through the window onto the roof. The wooden shingles were slippery with frost and cold on my bare feet. To keep from slipping, I crawled on all fours and leaned out to peer around the corner of the house. Something in the yard was flickering, and that could mean only one thing—fire!

The next moment I was pounding on my parents' door and when I opened it, I could see through their window onto the barnyard. The tractor shed was a blaze of light.

Dad climbed out of bed and pulled on his overalls over his pyjamas in a single motion. "Get your clothes on, Jon," he snapped, and then pounded off like fury down the stairs.

I grabbed my own chore clothes and headed for the kitchen where Mom was at the telephone calling for help. Snatching up my boots and jacket, I slammed out the door and had the good sense to take two empty milk pails with me.

Dad was silhouetted against the shed, a pail of water in each hand. He'd managed to open the shed door, but a single glance told me we were too late to save the tractor. Inside, the shed was a sheet of flames. Dad threw his water at it, but with no effect.

"The hay!" I shouted, pointing to the stacks just behind the shed. Sparks were landing at the foot of the first stack and partway up it.

"Get more water!" my father called, and we ran for the trough in the corral. By the time we'd filled our four pails, it was almost empty. The river, our next source of water, was ninety metres away.

The haystack was beginning to smolder. I threw my water at it and ran for the river, meeting Dad on his way back with slopping pails. "Hurry!" he gasped. "If the stacks catch, the fire could spread to the barn, too."

By the time I was back, Mom was outside, holding some old blankets. She grabbed one of my pails, soaked a blanket, and then aimed it at the sparks.

Dad ran up again with two more sloshing pails. "Jon!" he shouted, "Get up on the stack." He handed me another dripping blanket, yelling that I should beat out the sparks!

I scrambled up onto the hay and beat at smoldering spots and then stamped with my feet as well. I could really feel the heat through my boots.

Just then, with a sudden roar, the shed roof collapsed. Blazing shingles flew in all directions, and Mom screamed as one landed at her feet. "Get it!" I shouted and then ducked as several more blew past me, like falling stars. A dozen or more shingles landed on the haystack.

I kicked at two shingles, but they fell short, landing in the hay again. Without thinking, I grabbed a third one in my hand and tossed it toward Mom, who wrapped it in the blanket.

I grabbed another shingle—burning, too—but I didn't feel anything. My father was below me, and I threw it toward him and then beat at the hay with my wet blanket.

Down the road I half glimpsed a set of lights in the distance and knew it would be the Woloshyns or the Gunnarsons, our nearest neighbours. The fire truck couldn't possibly be here already.

The Woloshyns's truck screeched up and stopped with a jolt beside the barn. A moment later, Pete Woloshyn was up on the second stack, and his brother, Joseph, was using a pitchfork to move blazing piles of hay to one side.

"Get more water!" Joseph shouted, and Dad ran for the river just as two more vehicles arrived. Three more people clambered out carrying empty pails and followed my father to the river.

Dad ran up with his pails and handed them to Pete, while someone else handed water to me and I poured it where it was needed. Perhaps we could win this battle after all!

Suddenly the yard was full of trucks and cars and people. A bucket brigade was started from the river to the stacks, and before long we had both haystacks under control, with the exception of one fiery pile that the men had pitchforked some distance away.

I slid down off the stack and went over to Dad, who was standing in front of the flaming shed, his shoulders slumped. I could read his thoughts—he was wondering where he would get the money for a new tractor.

At that moment, the fire truck roared up, lights flashing. Two yellow-clad men began pumping water on the shed. When the tanks were empty, someone drove the fire truck to the river for more water.

"Go and see if your mother needs help in the house," Dad said to me. "Tell her we'll be ready for coffee soon."

My jacket was a mess, soaked and blackened, and there were two small holes burned in the leg of my overalls. When I glanced at my hands, I wished I hadn't. I'd been too busy to feel them before, but there were big blisters where I'd grabbed burning shingles, and several fingers were swollen. They were really beginning to hurt now that I was focusing on them.

When Mom saw my hands, she gasped, and the next moment she had me sitting on a chair, soaking them in a basin of cool water. "You should have put on gloves," she muttered as she used a cloth to wipe off the soot. "Look at your face, too."

Her own face was still smudged with smoke, and her hair looked frizzled. "The men will be in soon for coffee," I told her.

Later everyone took a look at my burns, and Mom hunted up some ointment and bandaged my hands. That helped a little, but they still hurt a lot.

"How did you happen to notice the fire, Jon?" Dad asked. "How come you were awake? If you hadn't seen it, we'd have lost everything—maybe even the house."

83

"It was Dandy," I said. "She climbed up on the veranda roof and meowed at my window. When I opened it, she kept on yowling until I went out on the roof to get her. And then I saw some light flickering," I finished, "so that's when I called you."

"So, it was the cat who saved your barn," Pete said. "You'd better give her a good drink of milk in the morning."

The neighbours soon headed for home. Before the firefighters left, they inspected all around one last time, and Dad checked over the whole area, too. Mom sent me to bed.

My room was cold, as I'd left the window wide open in my hurry to call Dad. There was another surprise, too—lying at the foot of my bed was Dandy, who must have come in the window while we were outside fighting the fire. When I crawled into bed, she curled up beside my shoulder, purring loudly.

My hands hurt, and I had trouble falling asleep. I heard the last of the neighbours leave and my parents talking downstairs for a long time. Then I must have dozed off, because I didn't hear Dad open my door. I roused enough to see him standing beside my bed though, and in the faint light from the hallway, I saw him reach out and stroke Dandy several times. The purring got louder.

MEDIA WATCH

Look for news stories about rescues. What do you notice about stories that get the most attention?

DIG DEEPER

1. What can you *infer* about the narrator's personality from what he says and does in this story? Make a chart listing at least two personality or character traits. Give evidence from the story.

Character traits	Evidence from the story

2. Imagine this story was rewritten to be a TV show. In a group, list what would change and what would stay the same.

MAX'S LOGBOOK

BY MARISSA MOSS

TONGS FOR PICKING GREEN THINGS OFF PIZZAS

TEST TUBES

HER NOTEBOOKS LOOK LIKE THIS. SHE MUST HAVE FILLED UP ABOUT 20 BY NOW!

LITMUS PAPER

BUNSEN BURNER

AH! THE SMELL OF FRESH-COOKED CHEMICALS

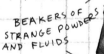
BEAKERS OF STRANGE POWDERS AND FLUIDS

THIS IS MY NEW LOGBOOK FOR WRITING SCIENTIFIC STUFF IN. MY MOM AND DAD ARE REAL SCIENTISTS, AND I'M WORKING ON BECOMING ONE, TOO. I GOT THE IDEA TO START THIS RECORD FROM A GIRL IN MY CLASS WHO KEEPS A NOTEBOOK ABOUT EVERYTHING IN HER LIFE.

SUPER BORING!

I WOULD NEVER, I MEAN NEVER, DO THAT, BUT I HAVE SO MANY GREAT IDEAS, I NEED A PLACE TO RECORD THEM. I DON'T WANT TO FORGET ANY OF MY COOL INVENTIONS OR EXPERIMENTS.

AT SCHOOL, WE MADE VOLCANOES AGAIN. HOW MANY TIMES DO WE HAVE TO MIX BAKING SODA AND VINEGAR? WHEN DO WE GET TO USE REAL CHEMICALS? DAD SAYS WHEN HE WAS A KID, YOU COULD GET ALL KINDS OF COOL STUFF YOU CAN'T BUY ANYMORE.

How can writing down our feelings help us to deal with life's problems?

I WANTED TO MAKE THINGS MORE INTERESTING THAN THE SAME OLD VOLCANO, SO WE MADE A GROUP OF ERASER PEOPLE TRYING TO FLEE THE BURNING LAVA.

SHOCKED, PANICKY ERASER PEOPLE
↓

OMAR LOVED THE IDEA, BUT OUR TEACHER, MS. BLODGE, DIDN'T THINK IT WAS FUNNY — OR EDUCATIONAL.

WE PUT THOSE ERASERS AWAY FAST. BUT I'M GOING TO GET MORE AND MAKE A WHOLE ARMY NEXT TIME. OMAR WANTS TO MAKE ERASER ALIENS. I TOLD HIM WE CAN DO BOTH.

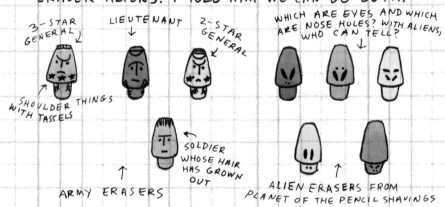

3-STAR GENERAL ↓

LIEUTENANT ↓

2-STAR GENERAL ↓

WHICH ARE EYES AND WHICH ARE NOSE HOLES? WITH ALIENS, WHO CAN TELL? ↓

SHOULDER THINGS WITH TASSELS

SOLDIER WHOSE HAIR HAS GROWN OUT ←

↑ ARMY ERASERS

ALIEN ERASERS FROM PLANET OF THE PENCIL SHAVINGS

AS BORING AS SCHOOL IS, SOME DAYS IT'S A LOT BETTER THAN BEING AT HOME. KEVIN STAYS IN HIS ROOM WITH HIS HEADPHONES ON, SO HE DOESN'T NOTICE, BUT I DO. I CAN'T HELP BUT HEAR MOM AND DAD YELLING. LAST NIGHT THERE WAS LOTS OF DOOR SLAMMING, TOO. THIS MORNING, DAD HAD ALREADY GONE TO WORK WHEN I GOT UP, BUT I COULD SEE FROM MOM'S SWOLLEN, RED EYES THAT SHE'D BEEN CRYING.

That evening...

Now I <u>KNOW</u> I HAVE SOMETHING TO WORRY ABOUT. MOM AND DAD CALLED A FAMILY MEETING FOR TONIGHT. WE HAVEN'T HAD A FAMILY MEETING SINCE I ACCIDENTALLY BROKE THE KITCHEN WINDOW. IT'S GOT TO BE SOMETHING <u>SERIOUS</u>.

I TRIED TO EAT DINNER, BUT THE MEATBALLS FELT LIKE LEAD BALLS.

THE APPLESAUCE WAS LIKE CEMENT, AND THE RICE TASTED LIKE GRITTY SAND.

IT WASN'T A MEAL, IT WAS CONSTRUCTION MATERIAL.

I COULD TELL MOM AND DAD WERE NERVOUS. KEVIN LOOKED NERVOUS, TOO. THEIR NERVOUSNESS MADE <u>ME</u> EVEN MORE NERVOUS. THE AIR IN THE ROOM FELT LIKE A RUBBER BAND THAT HAD BEEN S T R E T C H E D TIGHT AND WAS ABOUT TO SNAP.

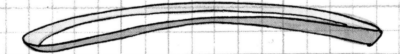

AND THEN THE SNAP CAME — MOM SAID WE MUST HAVE NOTICED SOME TENSION BETWEEN HER AND DAD (KEVIN AND I SAID NOTHING), AND THEY HAD DECIDED IT WOULD BE BETTER FOR THEM TO SEPARATE.

DAD SAID HE'D ALREADY FOUND AN APARTMENT AND
WOULD MOVE OUT THIS WEEKEND. WE'RE SUPPOSED TO STAY
WITH MOM DURING THE WEEK, AND EVERY OTHER WEEKEND
WE'LL STAY WITH DAD.

DAD TRIED TO BE NICE ABOUT IT. "WE'RE STILL A
FAMILY," HE SAID. "I'LL ALWAYS BE YOUR DAD." BUT
THAT'S NOT MY IDEA OF A FAMILY, NOT MY IDEA OF
A DAD.

THEN WE HAD A STIFF FAMILY HUG.

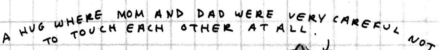
A HUG WHERE MOM AND DAD WERE VERY CAREFUL NOT
TO TOUCH EACH OTHER AT ALL.

DAD LOOKED
MISERABLE.

KEVIN
STARED
STRAIGHT
AHEAD, HIS
FACE A BLANK.

ME, I DIDN'T
KNOW WHERE
TO LOOK OR WHAT
TO FEEL.

MOM LOOKED
AT THE FLOOR.

IT WAS THE WORST NIGHT OF MY LIFE.

BLACK CLOUDS OF WORRY TURNED TO BLACK CLOUDS OF DOOM.

The next day...

I WANTED TO TELL OMAR WHAT WAS WRONG, BUT I COULDN'T. MAYBE IF NOBODY KNOWS MY DAD HAS MOVED OUT, IT HASN'T REALLY HAPPENED. MAYBE I IMAGINED THE WHOLE THING. MAYBE I'VE INVENTED SOME WEIRD ALTERNATIVE REALITY I'M STUCK IN. MAYBE.

OMAR LINED UP HIS ALIEN ERASERS, AND I TRIED TO PLAY WITH HIM, BUT HE COULD TELL I WASN'T REALLY PAYING ATTENTION.

THEN CLASS STARTED AND THINGS GOT WORSE. MS. BLODGE WAS MAD I HADN'T TURNED IN MY HOMEWORK (YEAH, YEAH, I FORGOT IT), AND SHE SAID I'D HAVE TO STAY INSIDE DURING RECESS TO FINISH IT. SO I STAYED INSIDE. BUT I DIDN'T DO MY HOMEWORK. I WORKED ON THE COMIC INSTEAD.

MOM GOT HOT CHOCOLATE AND DOUGHNUTS FOR KEVIN AND
ME AFTER SCHOOL. SHE'S NEVER DONE THAT BEFORE. THEN I DID
MY HOMEWORK (YES, MS. BLODGE, ALL OF IT!) BEFORE DAD
CAME TO TAKE ME AND KEVIN OUT FOR PIZZA.

IT'S LIKE BOTH MOM AND DAD ARE BEING NICE WITH FOOD BECAUSE
IT'S THE ONLY WAY THEY CAN BE NICE RIGHT NOW.
↓

SWEET DOUGHNUT-
TOO SWEET AND DOUGHY
TODAY

PEPPERONI PIZZA - USUALLY MY
FAVOURITE, BUT IT DIDN'T TASTE RIGHT
SOMEHOW

WE ATE PIZZA AND TOLD BAD JOKES, AND THINGS ALMOST
FELT NORMAL. ALMOST, I KEPT TELLING MYSELF. UNTIL DAD
DROPPED US BACK AT THE HOUSE LIKE HE'D JUST BEEN
GIVING US A RIDE AND WASN'T PART OF OUR FAMILY, REALLY.
THERE WAS NO PRETENDING NORMAL THEN, AND THINGS GOT
REALLY WEIRD. DAD HUGGED KEVIN AND ME, AND I COULD
SEE HE WAS CRYING.

SO I WHISPERED IN HIS EAR, "DON'T WORRY, DAD, WE'LL
INVENT ANOTHER KIND OF FAMILY." AND WE WILL. I KNOW
WE WILL.

IF YOU TAKE APART A FAMILY, CAN YOU PUT IT BACK TOGETHER
IN A WAY THAT MAKES SENSE?

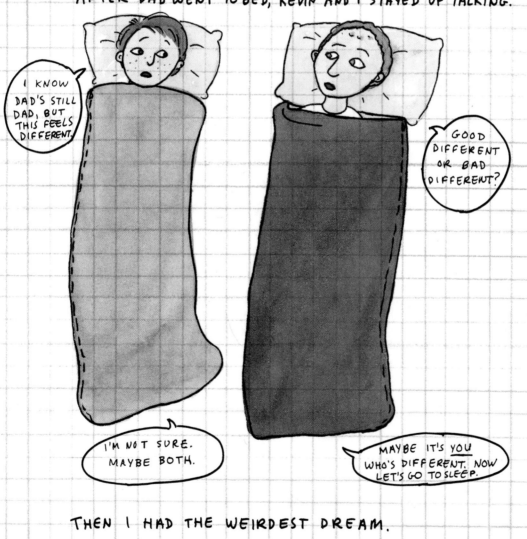

DAD'S PLACE WASN'T WHAT I'D IMAGINED. IT WAS SMALL AND MOSTLY EMPTY, LIKE A DOCTOR'S WAITING ROOM — NO SOCKS ANYWHERE THAT I COULD SEE. WE PLAYED CARDS AND ATE POPCORN, BUT EVEN THAT DIDN'T MAKE IT FEEL COZIER.

AFTER DAD WENT TO BED, KEVIN AND I STAYED UP TALKING.

I KNOW DAD'S STILL DAD, BUT THIS FEELS DIFFERENT.

GOOD DIFFERENT OR BAD DIFFERENT?

I'M NOT SURE. MAYBE BOTH.

MAYBE IT'S YOU WHO'S DIFFERENT. NOW LET'S GO TO SLEEP.

THEN I HAD THE WEIRDEST DREAM.

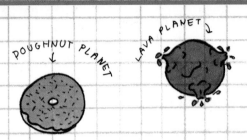
POUGHNUT PLANET

LAVA PLANET

FINGERPRINT PLANET

WRINKLE PLANET

ALL MY ALIEN ERASERS WERE ALIVE, AND THEY WERE SHOWING ME THEIR PLANETS. IT WAS A GALACTIC TOUR, KIND OF. EACH PLACE WAS COOL IN A DIFFERENT WAY.

PINEAPPLE PLANET

HAPPY FACE PLANET

PUMPKIN PLANET

SPIKEY PLANET

ROTTEN PLANET

THEN I CAME TO A PLANET THAT WAS PERFECT FOR ME, FULL OF INVENTIONS AND EXPERIMENTAL STUFF. AND I KNEW THAT WAS WHERE I BELONGED. IN FRONT OF ME, I SAW TWO DOORS.

ONE LED TO MY BEDROOM.

THE OTHER OPENED INTO DAD'S NEW APARTMENT.
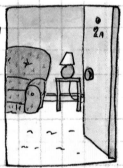

I WASN'T SURE WHICH DOOR TO GO THROUGH. DID I HAVE TO CHOOSE ONE OR THE OTHER? I COULDN'T DECIDE.
A VOICE SUDDENLY BOOMED OUT.

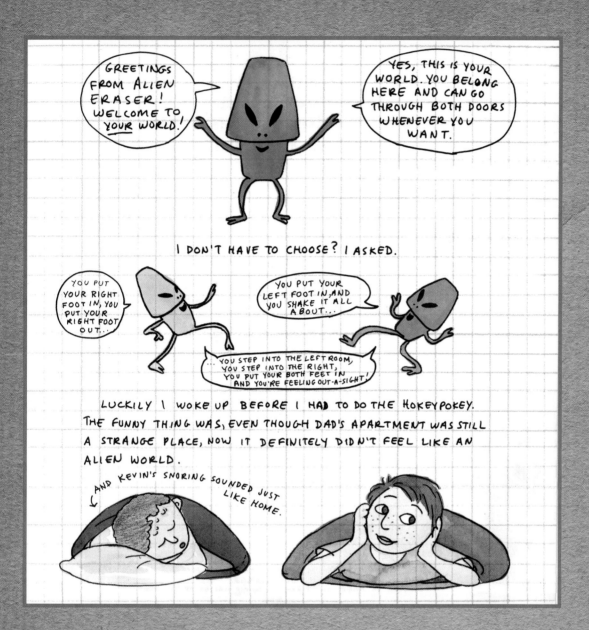

93

DIG DEEPER

1. Make a web or mind map to show other characters or stories from books, TV shows, or movies that you connect with Max.

2. With a partner, write a logbook entry by Max six months after the last entry in the story. Use words and pictures to describe how things have worked out for Max and his family.

Fiction Writers at Work!

No matter what form a story takes, it always starts with an idea in the writer's mind. What ideas do you have that are waiting to grow into stories? You are going to create a fictional story that is true-to-life—a realistic story.

Plan Your Story

- Who is your audience? How do you want them to react when they read your story? What do you want them to feel, think, and remember?

- Decide what form your story will take. Will it be a short story, TV script, or graphic story?

- Make a story map. Include the setting, characters, problem, main events, and solution.

FINDING STORY IDEAS

Use one or more of these strategies to help you get started.

- Browse through your Writer's Notebook.
- Think about stories you like to read.
- Use an experience from your own life.
- Start with a conflict or problem.
- Invent an unusual character.

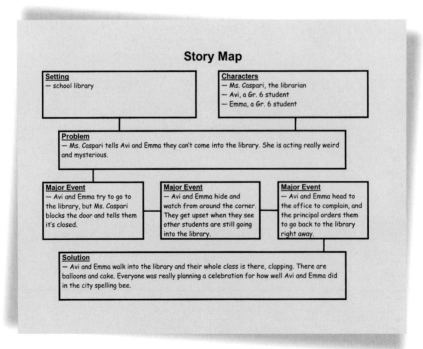

Story Map

Setting
— school library

Characters
— Ms. Caspari, the librarian
— Avi, a Gr. 6 student
— Emma, a Gr. 6 student

Problem
— Ms. Caspari tells Avi and Emma they can't come into the library. She is acting really weird and mysterious.

Major Event
— Avi and Emma try to go to the library, but Ms. Caspari blocks the door and tells them it's closed.

Major Event
— Avi and Emma hide and watch from around the corner. They get upset when they see other students are still going into the library.

Major Event
— Avi and Emma head to the office to complain, and the principal orders them to go back to the library right away.

Solution
— Avi and Emma walk into the library and their whole class is there, clapping. There are balloons and cake. Everyone was really planning a celebration for how well Avi and Emma did in the city spelling bee.

Write a Draft

- Decide who will tell the story.
- Try to start with an interesting event.
- Give each of your characters a unique voice.

Revise

- Read your story, thinking about ways to improve it. Make changes that make sense to you.
- Decide on two aspects where feedback from other students would help. Ask at least two people for advice on each.

Present Your Story

- Decide how you will present your story. You might record it, put it in the class library or on the school Web site, or have a group perform it as a drama or Readers' Theatre.

CHOOSING A NARRATOR

Who will narrate your story? Will you tell it

- in the voice of one of the characters? (What insights into the story might this person have? What might this person *not* know about the story?)
- from the point of view of someone who is not part of the story?

Horse and Train
by Alex Colville

What story might there
be behind the meeting of
a horse and a train?

DIG DEEPER ....

1. Make two-column notes to describe the
   painting and your response to it. In the first
   column, describe what you see in the
   painting. In the second column, record your
   feelings, reactions, and questions.

2. With a partner, create *two* pictures showing
   what might have happened *before* the
   painting. Create a soundtrack to go with
   your pictures and the actual painting.

96

VIEW LIKE AN ARTIST
How does the artist draw the viewer's eyes toward the train?

97

GOOD READS!

LOOKING FOR A GOOD BOOK?

Here are three Canadian authors who write about real kids. Some of their books are funny; others are serious or suspenseful. But they are all good reads.

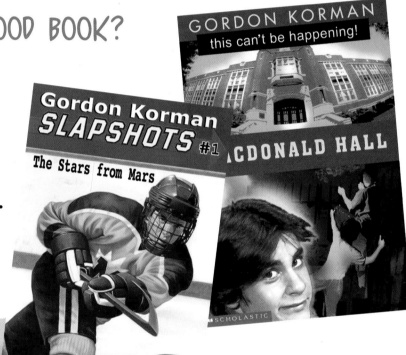

GORDON KORMAN
this can't be happening!

Gordon Korman
SLAPSHOTS #1
The Stars from Mars

MACDONALD HALL

SCHOLASTIC

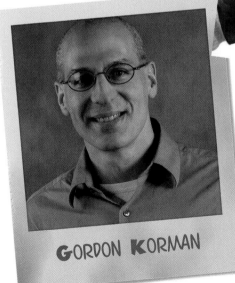

GORDON KORMAN

GORDON KORMAN wrote his first book, *This Can't Be Happening*, when he was in Grade 7! Since then, he has written over 50 books for kids and has become one of the best known writers for young people in the world. Here is what one young reader thought about Book One of Korman's adventure series, *Everest*.

Everest, Book One: The Contest

Reviewed by Irene

Are you competitive? If so, you may enjoy this story about some athletic, ambitious teenagers.

This story begins with Dominic, a 13-year-old mountain climber who wins a chance to compete for a place on the first kids' expedition to climb Mount Everest. He and nine other competitors arrive at the training camp in High Falls, Colorado. They have to practise climbing for many hours every day. Cap Cicero, their coach and judge, eliminates climbers regularly. Sleep is disturbed by loud crashes in the night. The story has some mysteries because there is a suspected spy and a vandal.

The story focuses on team building. It shows how teenagers argue, play, and help each other. I like this story because I like the mystery and adventure. I really admire Cap Cicero and Dominic because they are kind and brave, and Cap Cicero is a good leader.

The most exciting part is when one of the climbers, Brynn, falls. It is very dark, extremely cold, and the weather is ugly. Cap Cicero and his team work together to try to rescue Brynn. She is badly injured and unconscious, so she can't help herself.

If you want to read a book about an exciting adventure, this is a good book for you.

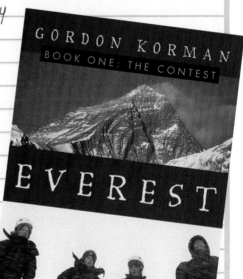

READ LIKE A WRITER

How does the reviewer show you that she is excited about the book?

RACHNA GILMORE

RACHNA GILMORE grew up in India and England. She moved to Prince Edward Island in the 1970s and now lives in Ottawa. Gilmore has written books for young children and adults, as well as for middle readers. In 1999, one of her stories won the Governor General's Literary Award for children's literature. In the following interview, Gilmore describes her writing process.

WHERE DO YOU GET YOUR IDEAS?

RG: Ideas come from a huge variety of places, from ordinary life, from all around me. It may be something I've seen that gets me wondering, or something I've read that spins me in a new direction. Sometimes it's just a feeling about a place. The only thing that matters about an idea is that I have to be really, *really* interested in it. It has to seize my imagination and heart so that I just *have to* explore it.

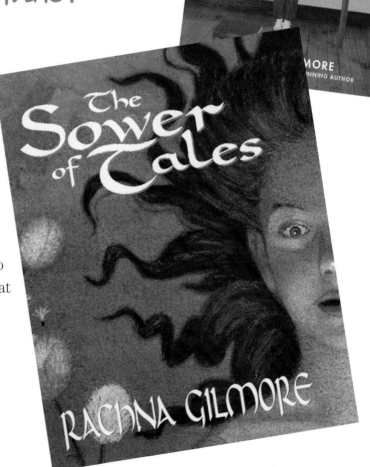

HOW LONG DOES IT TAKE YOU TO WRITE A BOOK?

RG: It usually takes at least six months to a year, and sometimes several years. That's from beginning to end, right from when that first idea seizes me and won't let go. Once I get an idea I'm really interested in, I have to brainstorm for other ideas that fit. It's a bit like putting together a puzzle. When I have a sense of what the story is about, I play with it in my head until I know the voice of the main character—know what she is like and what she's feeling.

When I think I have the overall shape of the story and the voice of the main character, I write it down fast. I don't worry about spelling or grammar or punctuation. I want to capture the heart of the story and the feelings.

After the first draft comes the real work. That's when I have to look at the story over and over, think about it, make sure it's the best it can be, and rewrite it as many times as it takes. This can often take months because after each draft, I have to put the story away for a while so that I can come back to it with fresh eyes.

JACQUELINE GUEST

JACQUELINE GUEST is a Métis writer who lives in Alberta. Some of her books explore Métis history; others focus on kids who play sports. Her characters have to deal with problems in life and on the field or in the arena. They face issues such as bullying, physical challenges, fairness, and blended families. The stories are always fast paced, realistic, and very readable.

In *A Goal in Sight*, the main character, Aiden, is an enforcer on a hockey team—and a bully off the ice, as well. But Aiden secretly wants to do more than just fight other players. He feels he has it in him to score goals. In the excerpt on the next page, he's been told to cover another player, Jamie, who is the star forward on the team.

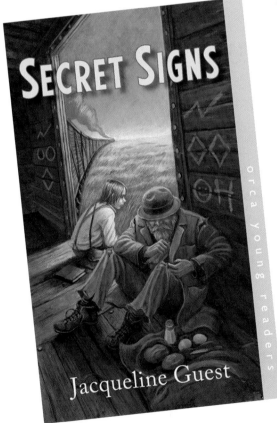

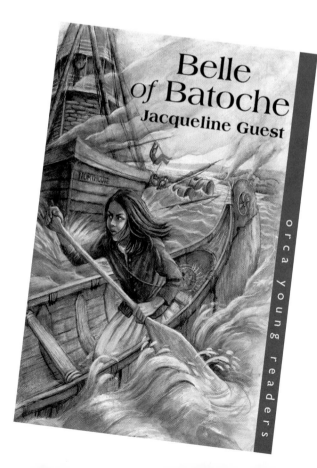

Aiden moved up beside Jamie. "Pass me the puck. I know how to get it past their goalie!" he shouted.

"I'm taking this one in, Aiden. Give me some protection!" Jamie yelled back.

Aiden didn't want to give him any protection. He wanted to score a goal. "I said give me the puck!" he yelled, lifting Jamie's stick and stealing the puck for himself...

The goalie was still standing wrong and when he went for Aiden's low fake shot, he overbalanced and fell to his knees. Before he could spring back up, Aiden fired a sizzler, top right corner. The goal light whirled!

Aiden punched the air and shook his stick. Winner! Satisfied he'd done a great job, he headed for the bench.

"What do you think you're doing, Walsh?" Coach Goldstein asked the second Aiden came through the gate. "Your job is to cover the shooters, which means running tough interferences for Jamie, not stripping the puck and going for the glory yourself. On this team, players follow team orders."

Aiden stopped, confused. He should have been getting congratulations, not this. The happiness he'd just felt evaporated into the chilly air.

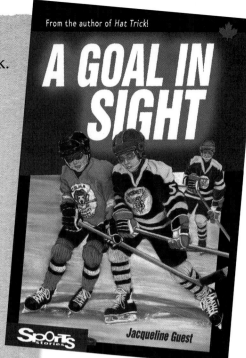

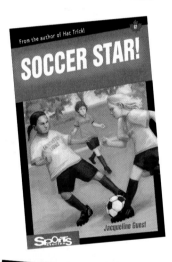

DIG DEEPER

1. What makes a good novel? In a group, identify the top five criteria you use to judge a novel. Give examples of novels that meet your criteria.

2. Choose a favourite book or movie that tells a realistic story and write a short review modelled after the one on page 99.

103

PEANUTS

How does a writer create a plot?

PEANUTS® featuring "Good ol' Charlie Brown" by Schulz

It was a dark and stormy night.

Suddenly, a shot rang out. A door slammed. The maid screamed.

Suddenly, a pirate ship appeared on the horizon!

While millions of people were starving, the king lived in luxury.

Meanwhile, on a small farm in Kansas, a boy was growing up.

Part II

IN PART TWO, I TIE ALL OF THIS TOGETHER..

DIG DEEPER

1. With a group, brainstorm some ways Snoopy's story might end.
2. Create another comic strip in which Snoopy gives advice on how to write an exciting plot.

The Cello of Mr. O

by JANE CUTLER

Illustrated by GREG COUCH

How can music help in a time of war?

Here we are, surrounded and under attack.

My father and most of the other fathers, the older brothers—even some of the grandfathers—have gone to fight. So we stay, children and women, the old and the sick, managing as best we can.

I am afraid almost all the time.

At night, from my window, I can see the white trails of tracer fire and the orange flash of mortars in the sky. I pretend I am watching shooting stars and meteors.

The streets of our city are littered with bricks, dust, and broken glass. We have no heating oil. Last winter, we slept in our clothes in the kitchen, next to a sheet-metal stove Papa put together before he left.

We used up all our wood. If something doesn't change by the time winter comes again, we will have to burn furniture and books to keep warm.

Food is scarce, of course. And water. We collect rainwater in bowls and buckets. And we go to distribution centres and bring water home.

Some people carry their heavy containers of water in shopping carts, some in wheelbarrows. In winter, many of us use sleds. Last week, Mama and I saw a woman hauling water in a wheelchair.

Each Wednesday at four, the relief truck comes to a street right outside our square. We wait in line to receive soap, cooking oil, canned fish, flour.

Nothing is as it was: shops, cars, and apartments have been destroyed. Schools are closed, the electricity is usually out, and there is no gas at all. Even the telephones don't work.

Many people have left.

Some, like Mama's friend Marya, stay because they have no place else to go. And some, like my mother, have decided to stay—no matter what.

Mama can't stand the idea of Papa coming back to nothing. She
wants us to be here.

Mama sighs. "This is not the first time in history that such a
thing has happened," she tells me.

It may not be the first time it has happened. But it is the first
time it has happened to me.

I am angry almost all the time.

My friends and I stay close to home, usually inside our large
apartment building, sitting under the stairs. We pass the time playing
cards and word games. Reading books. Drawing. Talking. We imagine
what we would have if we could eat whatever we wanted.

Sometimes we can't sit still a minute longer, and we run through the halls, laughing and making noise.

Then Mr. O flings open his door. "Quiet, you kids!" he shouts. As if kids were a bad thing.

When the relief truck comes at four o'clock on Wednesdays, everyone goes into the street. It feels like a party, being outside with so many other people for a change.

Even Mr. O stands in line.

But he doesn't chat. He just waits, looking away from the rest of us.

"A thinker," my mother says quietly, nodding in his direction.

"A thinker," her friend Marya says, but in a mocking tone.

Marya doesn't agree with my mother. Neither do I.

Mr. O isn't thinking. He is just being unfriendly.

We children don't like Mr. O. Whenever one of us can find a paper bag, we blow it up with air and then pop it right outside his apartment door. It sounds just like a shell exploding!

We laugh and run, imagining his fear.

When he is not waiting in line for supplies with the rest of us, Mr. O plays his cello.

It is a fine cello, one of the best. My father, who loves music, too—who plays tender songs and lively tunes on the harmonica—told me this about the cello of Mr. O.

"The front and the back of that excellent cello were carved out of German fiddleback maple and hand-rubbed with a special polish made in France," said my father.

"The neck of the cello was made of mahogany from Honduras, and the fingerboard of ebony, probably from Ceylon," he said.

"As for the bow," my father continued, "it was carved out of a soft wood that grows in Brazil. The ivory on its tip came from Africa."

"People all over the world had to cooperate to make the cello of Mr. O," my father said.

My father told me about Mr. O, too. "When he was young, he travelled around the world, playing his cello in great halls for hundreds of people who cheered when he finished, and threw flowers."

If my father knew about the paper bags, he would be angry.

But Papa is far away, fighting somewhere in the mountains. He has taken his harmonica and all his warm clothes with him, and we have no idea when we will see him again.

It is four o'clock in the afternoon, a dull fall Wednesday. My friend Elena and I are playing jacks under the stairs. We hear the supply truck roar up. But we are lazy, and for once, we don't rush outside to wait with the others.

We hear the footsteps of people leaving their apartments, leaving the building.

We hear the murmur of talk and laughter.

Then we hear the rocket hit.

The truck is destroyed. Some people we know are badly hurt.

Now, even though we clear away the rubble and smooth over the ground, supplies will not be brought here. We are too easy a target, they tell us. Now we will have to walk for kilometres to get anything, and nothing will happen to make even one day a week better than the others.

But on the first Wednesday after the rocket, at exactly four o'clock, Mr. O appears, all dressed up, carrying his cello, carrying a chair.

He marches out into the middle of the square, where everyone can see him.

He sets up his chair.

He takes out his cello.

He tightens his horsehair bow and rubs it with rosin.

Then he takes a deep breath.

He plays.

"The music of Bach," Mama tells me, her face shining, as we listen to the complicated music, the powerful and reassuring notes.

How he plays, our Mr. O! As if he were on the stage of a grand, warm hall, playing for people who will throw flowers. As if he were not alone in the centre of a deserted square in a besieged city, where even a relief truck will no longer come.

"They will kill him!" Marya cries fearfully.

"They would not bother to kill an old man playing a cello," Mama says.

I am not so sure.

Because the music of the cello makes us feel less angry. And the courage of the cellist makes us less afraid.

If they guess, it could be reason enough for them to want to stop the music, which feeds us as truly as the supplies brought by the truck did.

Mr. O does not play only on Wednesdays. Every day at four o'clock, he and his cello appear.

One day, after he has started playing, Mr. O gets a cramp in his leg. He leans the cello against his chair and hobbles about, shaking his leg.

We hear a fusillade of exploding shells.

We see clouds of black smoke.

Finally, when the smoke clears, we see that the cellist is unharmed. But all that remains of the cello is splintered wood and tangled strings.

What will feed us now? I wonder.

It is the very next day that I find the brown paper bag. It is a small one, and crumpled. I smooth it out as best I can. Then I put it under Papa's heavy dictionary and leave it there all night.

In the morning, I choose the best crayons I have from the cigar box where I keep them. Most of them are now just stubs of crayons. Still, I have many different colours left.

Carefully, on the crinkly paper bag, I draw. I draw a picture of Mr. O in his dark suit sitting on a chair, playing a cello. Then I draw bright flowers falling all around him.

When I finish, I take the picture and tiptoe up to Mr. O's apartment. I press my ear against the door and listen. Silence. Carefully, quietly, I slip the picture underneath the door. And then I run.

To everyone's surprise, promptly at four o'clock that afternoon, out of the building comes Mr. O, carrying a chair.

He sees me at my window, and he bows to me and smiles.

Then, from the pocket of his coat, he draws a small, shiny object. A harmonica!

From then on, for one hour every single day, Mr. O sits in the square and plays his harmonica.

The melodies sound sad and sweet and small, and very different from the grand songs Mr. O played on his cello.

"It is Bach, nevertheless," Mama says.

The music makes us feel happy.

And the courage of the harmonica player makes us less afraid.

DIG DEEPER ··

1. Summarize the story in a story map or a set of illustrated storyboards.
2. What do you think the writer wants her readers to think about or remember from this story? Give reasons and evidence for your answer.

River Friendly
River Wild

by Jane Kurtz • Illustrated by Neil Brennan

Sandbagging—April 12

Snow's melting,

river's rising,

water's coming from the south

like a pickup truck in overdrive.

Everybody's bagging sand.

Piling the bags on top of the dikes.

One, lift, two swing, three, catch, four, toss.

The water creeps into Sarah's yard.

The water creeps up to Sarah's back porch.

A truck rumbles by with sandbags for Sarah.

One, lift, two, swing, three, catch, four, toss.

A truck rumbles up to dump sand for Sarah.

Scrape, scritch, shovel the sand.

Swish, thump, drop it in the bag.

Wrist twist 'til the bag's closed.

Mom turns the wire to shut the bag's mouth.

One, lift, two, swing, three, catch, four, toss.

One, lift, two, swing, three, catch, four, toss.

READ LIKE A WRITER
How does the writer help readers see and hear what is happening?

How can a river be a character in a story?

Just in Case

At supper,

everyone is as quiet

as unturned pages in a book.

"Let's pack one bag," Mom says finally.

"Just one bag.

Just in case."

"Can I pack the cat?" I ask.

"If we *do* leave," Dad says,

"it will only be for a couple days.

She'd be much happier at home."

I pack

four books

three shirts

two pairs of jeans.

Then I lie in bed,

while my heart pumps

like a rowing machine.

Dad tucks me in.

"Promise me one thing, okay?" I say.

"Put out lots and lots and lots and lots

of food and water for Kiwi.

Just

in

case."

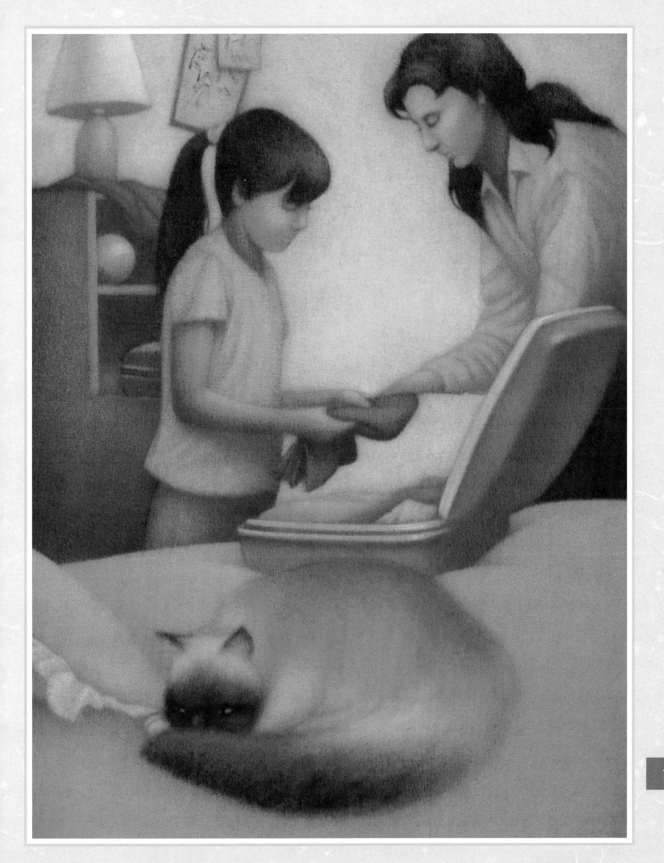

Fleeing–Just After Midnight–April 18

Most things you lie awake and worry about

don't happen.

This

one

does.

Sirens *woooo wooo* wake us up.

Woooo, wooooo.

Everybody out.

I cry over Kiwi.

Max kisses Kiwi.

We grab our bags.

Rush, rush, everybody out.

I blow kisses to Kiwi.

Max cries over Kiwi.

We rush—

hush—

through the midnight streets

out of the silent city

away from the river

away from our home.

Danger

The newspaper says:

Beware the river water.

It's contaminated with chemicals.

And be careful going back into your house.

The steps could be crumbled.

The floors could be buckled.

The stairs could be slick.

The windows could be broken,

and snakes could be inside.

We creep

up the steps

through the door.

"Kiwi?" I call.

No answer.

"Kitty, kitty," I call.

No cat.

I rumble around the two upstairs bedrooms

like a car that's lost its steering.

I creep down the slimy stairs.

My dad lifts a box and turns it over.

Water and paper dolls gush out.

The paper dolls

saw it all.

I wish they could tell me what happened to my cat.

"This was a great neighbourhood," Dad says.

"Old-fashioned," Mom says.

"You could borrow a cup of sugar

from anyone."

"Our next-door neighbour always brought in

our mail when we were gone," Max says.

"And fed Kiwi," I say.

We sit, trying to look at Mr. Ford's tulips

instead of the garbage piles.

The lawn is strewn with violets

and Mom's drying papers.

And then,

on careful feet,

around each paper

steps

a Kiwi cat.

DIG DEEPER

1. With a group, create an interesting presentation of one part of this poem. For example, you might include music or sound effects and have some students mime the characters' actions, while others read the words in a voice-over.

2. Write a poem about an event in your life. Use one part of this poem as a model. Try to use words that appeal to the senses.

Connect and Share

You have met some interesting fictional characters in this unit.
Now you are going to help bring them to life!

Gather your evidence!

- Choose a fictional character you read or talked about in this unit.

- Without naming the character, show what he or she is like by
    - designing a T-shirt the character might wear
    - choosing the character's favourite song
    - finding an object that might be important to the character

DESIGNING A T-SHIRT

Ask yourself these questions:

- What main impression would the character want to give others?
- What slogan or image might the character wear?
- What colour and type of lettering would add to the impact?

Share your challenge

- At home, display the three pieces of evidence to your family. Ask "What do these tell you about my character?" Compare their ideas with what you know about the character.

- At school, repeat the activity for your group or class. Then challenge them to name the character.

- Write a journal entry explaining how well your evidence worked.

Spotlight on **Learning**

Collect

■ Gather your notebooks, articles, pictures, and other work you did in this unit. Include your planning notes and reflections for oral activities.

Talk and reflect

Work with a partner.

■ Together, read the Learning Goals on page 64.

■ Talk about how well you met these goals.

■ Look through your work for evidence.

Select

■ Choose two pieces of work that show how you achieved the Learning Goals. (The same piece of work can show more than one goal.)

Tell about your choices

■ Tell what each piece shows about your learning.

My choices	I want this in my portfolio because...

Reflect

■ What have you learned about reading and viewing realistic fiction?

■ What have you discovered about techniques that authors, scriptwriters, and storytellers use?

123

UNIT 6

Exploring
Canada

LEARNING GOALS

In this unit you will

- Read and view fiction and non-fiction texts about the impact of early exploration in Canada.

- Analyze whose point of view is expressed.

- Research and write a news report about an event in Canadian history.

- Explore different versions of history through role playing and discussion.

Aboriginal peoples
early contact
cooperation
conflict
adventure
quest

Lost and Found

by Pat Hancock

Illustrated by Leanne Franson

How can objects tell stories about the past?

It was 1867. Fourteen-year-old Edward Lee had been working all morning with his father, John, to help clear fallen trees and stumps from a section of land just east of Cobden, Ontario. A local steamboat captain named Overman, who owned the property, had hired them to do the job. John chopped the tree trunks into smaller, more manageable logs. Then Edward used a pair of oxen to haul the logs away.

126

It should be lunchtime soon, Edward thought as he dug out some crumbly clay so he could slip a chain under a log. The log lay beside a small creek that ran into Green Lake.

When the oxen dragged off the log, Edward spied it—a yellow object glinting in the noonday sun.

Maybe it's a gold coin and I'll be rich, he thought wishfully as he knelt down to pull the metal disk free. It was round like a coin, but larger—about 15 cm across, with lines and numbers on it and an arm like an arrow attached at the centre.

"Pa, look what I found," Edward called to his father.

John put down his axe and joined his son.

"I think it's a compass," Edward said, handing him the brassy-looking disk.

"Maybe not, son, but it measures something. And did you notice this?" his father added, pointing to the small *1603* and *Paris* stamped on the dial-like face.

Edward did some quick mental arithmetic. "It's more than 250 years old, Pa! Maybe it's worth something."

"You never know," John said. "I'll see what the Captain has to say about it."

Later that day, Edward's father showed the object to Captain Overman, who asked to keep the piece, saying he'd give the Lees $10 for it.

This is the astrolabe Edward Lee found at Green Lake.

Fast-Forward

Overman never did pay the $10, and Edward later regretted letting his father hand over the object without getting the money first. Imagine how he might have felt if he had known that his discovery would one day be worth nearly 30 000 times that much!

The object Edward found was an astrolabe. Astrolabes were widely used for navigation from the third until the seventeenth century. They allowed sailors to figure out their location relative to the equator. Most astrolabes were melted down so the brass could be reused. Today, only 84 are known to exist worldwide.

Edward's find was very rare, but it's *where* he found the astrolabe that sparked the most interest and led to its great increase in value.

A painting of Samuel de Champlain

Flashback: 1613

In the spring of 1613, the famed French explorer Samuel de Champlain had just completed his fifth voyage across the Atlantic Ocean. An excellent navigator, Champlain kept daily journals and made detailed maps of the places he visited. On this trip, he decided to explore the Ottawa River for the first time.

Champlain's map. The red circle shows the Green Lake area.

It turned out to be a difficult trip. When he and his travelling companions reached the roiling rapids east of Grand Calumet Island, they had to abandon their canoes. The only way to continue was to portage inland across rough terrain toward Muskrat Lake. In his journal, Champlain mentions passing four small ponds on that portage. Some historians concluded that one of those ponds may have been Green Lake.

By the late 1800s, a few historians started wondering about the astrolabe Edward found in 1867. Could it have been Champlain's? Was it possible that the instrument slipped out of his pack as he clambered through the trees and bushes?

That possibility must have pleased R.W. Cassels of Toronto, the man who had received the astrolabe from Captain Overman. By 1901, news of its possible origins had spread. As a result, Cassels was able to sell it to Samuel Hoffman, an American, for $500. In 1942, Hoffman left it to the New York Historical Society in his will.

Home at Last

The astrolabe remained there until 1989. Then the newly completed Canadian Museum of Civilization paid the impressive sum of almost $300 000 and brought it home to Ottawa.

However, the instrument's original owner remains a mystery. Was it Champlain's astrolabe, or did it belong to missionaries who travelled along the same routes as Champlain? We may never know for sure, just as we may never know how and when it ended up in the spot Edward Lee found it so long ago.

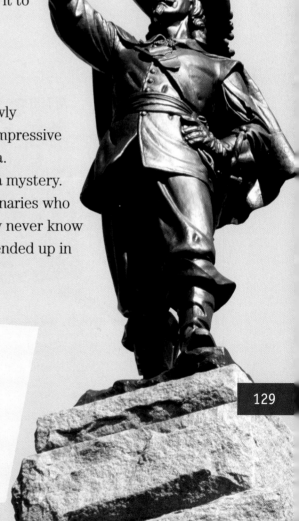

This statue of Champlain, erected in 1915, overlooks the Ottawa River. It shows Champlain holding an astrolabe. Unfortunately, he looks as if he doesn't know how to use the instrument—he's holding it upside down!

LET'S TALK ABOUT IT...

- In a small group, discuss what might have happened if Edward Lee had kept the astrolabe.
- Role-play a scene 200 years from now, in which someone uncovers an object from the early 21st century. What might the discoverer think it was?

Reading in Social Studies

Reading in Social Studies informs you about Aboriginal peoples and Canada's history. Reading about history can help you understand your world today.

TALK ABOUT IT!

Think about a person or event in early Canadian history.

- Why did this person or event catch your interest?

- Tell your partner why this person or event is important.

Here are some sources.

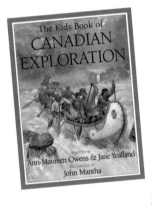

With a partner or group, make a web to record different resources about Aboriginal peoples and early Canadian history.

Multimedia ···· **Resources** ···· Visual

Print ···· Online

Think Like a Reader

Read with a purpose

- Why might you read about Aboriginal peoples and Canada's history?

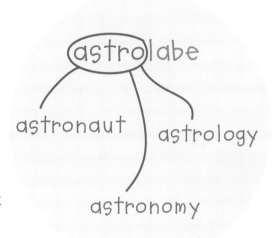

Crack the code

- When you come across a word you are not familiar with, think of other words that have similar parts.

Make meaning

Practise using these strategies when you read about history:

USE WHAT YOU KNOW   Look at the visuals and the headings. What do you already know about this topic?

DECIDE WHAT'S IMPORTANT   As you read, pick out important information.

SUMMARIZE   Organize the important information using a graphic organizer, such as a web or a chart.

Analyze what you read

- When you read about events that happened long ago, think about whose voices and points of view are *not* expressed.

- How can you tell if your source of information is reliable?

The Search for the Northwest Passage

To early explorers like John Cabot, North America was just one big roadblock. Explorers were looking for a shorter trade route to Asia and had no idea there was a continent in their way. Even after they realized what they had stumbled on, some explorers kept looking for a shortcut. By the late 16th century, they decided that the most likely route was through the North.

A Tough Job

If you look at a map of northern Canada, you will see how difficult their task was. The whole area is a maze of islands. Without a map, navigators couldn't tell where a waterway would lead. Sometimes ice broke boats into splinters. Many explorers died of starvation or disease, while others froze to death. Some simply disappeared.

USE WHAT YOU KNOW

What do you already know about the Northwest Passage?

132

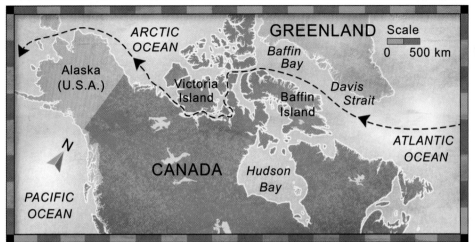

Roald Amundsen's route through the Northwest Passage (1903–1906)

DECIDE WHAT'S IMPORTANT

What are the key ideas about the search for the Northwest Passage?

Despite the risks, explorers were determined to find a route through the ice. Among the first to join the search were Martin Frobisher, John Davis, Henry Hudson, and William Baffin. Although none of these men succeeded, each added to Europeans' knowledge of the North. Frobisher Bay (now Iqaluit), Davis Strait, Hudson Bay, and Baffin Island were named after them.

The Second Wave

After 1650, interest in finding the passage began to fade, but in 1815 another generation of explorers took up the search. Among them were Edward Parry, John Franklin, and a Norwegian scientist, Roald Amundsen. In 1906, Amundsen became the first person to sail the Northwest Passage from east to west.

Because of the ice, the Northwest Passage was never used very much for trade. The explorers, however, learned a lot about the geography, resources, and peoples of the North. The English explorers learned that the Hudson Bay area was a perfect place to trade for furs, so they set up the Hudson's Bay Company. Soon this company controlled most of the fur trade in North America.

Henry Hudson made four attempts to find the Northwest Passage. On his last voyage in 1611, the crew mutinied. Hudson and his son were cast adrift in a small boat—never to be seen again.

SUMMARIZE

Arrange the main ideas and supporting details in a web.

133

Rivers as Roads

In the late 16th century, the most important fashion item for a European gentleman was a felt hat made of beaver fur. For over 200 years, the demand for beaver pelts drove the economy and growth of New France. The quest for furs also led people to explore regions of the continent they had never visited before.

USE WHAT YOU KNOW

What do you already know about the fur trade?

The Search for Furs

The fur trade was a great way to make money quickly. Many young men set out for the North Country to trade with the First Nations. Some were only teenagers. The French called these men *coureurs de bois* (runners of the woods).

Since there were no roads, the easiest way to travel was by water. Traders travelled the rivers and streams of Eastern and Central Canada. Some, like Louis Joliet, explored south into what is now the United States. Others, like Pierre de La Vérendrye and his sons, paddled west. They moved ever farther inland to explore the landscape and set up new fur-trading posts.

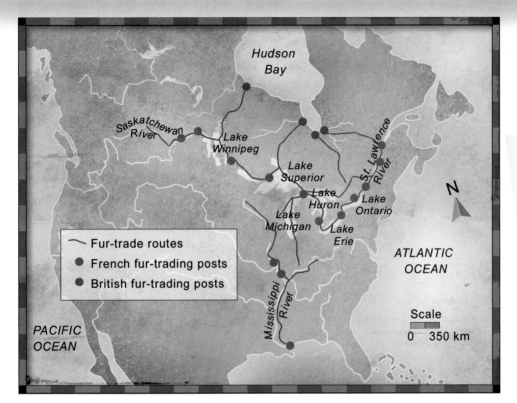

The network of French and British fur-trading posts in North America from 1600–1870

DECIDE WHAT'S IMPORTANT

What are the key ideas about the fur trade?

A Rough Life

The life of a coureur de bois was full of dangerous rapids, swarms of mosquitoes and blackflies, cold weather, and food shortages. These men travelled for months at a time and covered thousands of kilometres. They made friends with First Nations peoples, often living with them and learning their languages.

Many coureurs de bois married First Nations women. From them they learned how to build canoes and shelters from birch trees and which routes to use for portages. They also learned how to make preserved meat and berries called pemmican. Their children were the first Métis.

It was a hard life, but many were willing to put up with the discomforts and dangers. Working with First Nations, the coureurs de bois helped to draw the map of eastern and central parts of the continent.

This stamp of Etienne Brûlé was issued in 1987. Brûlé was 16 years old when he travelled to New France in 1608. He is often called the first coureur de bois.

SUMMARIZE

Arrange the main ideas and supporting details in a web.

135

Venturing Westward

For thousands of years, First Nations such as the Tlingit and the Haida were the only people living along the west coast of Canada. From time to time, Russian traders would visit from the North.

USE WHAT YOU KNOW

What do you already know about the exploration of Western Canada?

Explorers by Sea

In 1774, Spanish explorers arrived from Mexico to expand their trading routes. Many places in British Columbia are named after these early Spanish explorers—for example, the Strait of Juan de Fuca, Galiano Island, and Quadra Island.

Explorers from Europe had quite a challenge just getting to the area. The journey took a full year because ships had to sail around the southern tip of South America.

One explorer to make the trip was George Vancouver. He carefully charted the hundreds of inlets, bays, and islands along the coast, from present-day Vancouver Island to Alaska.

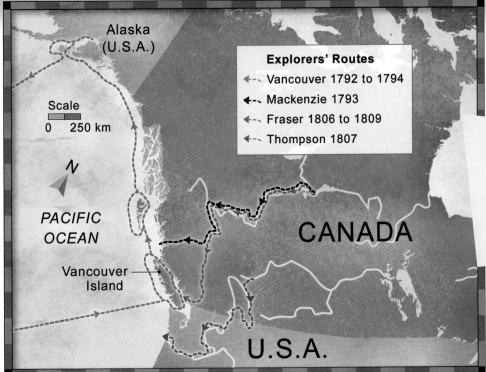

Exploring the West by land and sea

DECIDE WHAT'S IMPORTANT

What are the key ideas about venturing westward?

Although Vancouver's crew found him cold and distant, they must have respected his cartographic skills and his dedication.

Explorers by Land

Reaching the west coast by land took even longer because explorers had to cross the Rocky Mountains.

Alexander Mackenzie was the first European to make the journey. In 1793, he and his men travelled 1350 km, by canoe and on foot. It was a tough trip. Even Mackenzie realized it would never work as a trade route.

In 1807, David Thompson found an overland path through the mountains. Around the same time, Simon Fraser braved the rapids of what is now the Fraser River. He went all the way to the Pacific.

With each crossing, the map of the region took shape, and trade between East and West increased. By 1885, a new country would stretch from coast to coast to coast.

In 1778, James Cook (above) sailed up the Pacific coast. George Vancouver was a member of his crew.

SUMMARIZE

Arrange the main ideas and supporting details in a web.

137

Reflect on Your Reading

You have . . .

- talked about historical events.
- read about the causes and effects of exploration.
- used strategies to read challenging words.

astrolabe

coureur de bois

portage

cartographic

pemmican

venturing

I liked reading about the coureurs de bois. Their lives were so adventurous! What about you?

USE WHAT YOU KNOW

DECIDE WHAT'S IMPORTANT

SUMMARIZE

You have also . . .

- explored different reading strategies.

Write About Learning

How did using a graphic organizer help you summarize the information? What else could you have used to organize your summary? Write about how graphic organizers can help you read, understand, and remember information in Social Studies texts.

138

Read Like a Writer

When you were reading "Early Adventurers," you were reading *reports*. Report writers present information clearly and show how different facts or ideas are connected.

HINT!

Look at how the writer uses different **sentence patterns** to make the ideas flow smoothly.

TALK ABOUT IT!

Look at the reports you have read. Find a passage that you think is particularly clear or well written. Share it with a group.

- What do you notice about the sentences in this passage?

- How has the writer made connections among the facts or ideas?

- Make a chart showing what you have learned about writing sentences that flow.

To write sentences that flow
- combine related ideas from shorter sentences
- use a variety of sentence lengths and patterns
- connect ideas with transition words such as <u>because</u>, <u>when</u>, and <u>although</u>

139

Women Explorers

by Barbara Greenwood

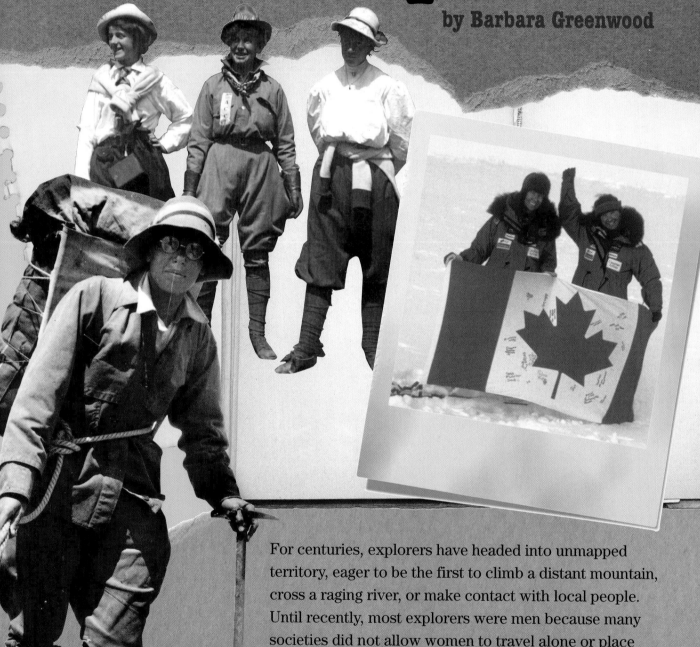

For centuries, explorers have headed into unmapped territory, eager to be the first to climb a distant mountain, cross a raging river, or make contact with local people. Until recently, most explorers were men because many societies did not allow women to travel alone or place themselves in danger. But there have always been some brave women who refused to be left behind.

140

How have women participated in exploration?

Gudrid: Early Adventurer

Around 1000 CE, a young Viking woman named Gudrid travelled to Greenland. There she married a wealthy merchant named Thorfinnr Karlsefni. Even though Greenland's climate at that time was mild enough for farming, the land was rocky, and the settlers often went hungry. When other Vikings told of better land to the southwest, Gudrid and Thorfinnr decided to find it. They joined sixty men and five women, travelling in two ships. They took cattle, tools, and other supplies they needed to start a colony.

The Vikings sailed to Helluland (Baffin Island) and then on to Markland (Labrador). When winter came, they stopped in a sheltered bay (possibly in Newfoundland), which they called Straumfjord. Here, Gudrid gave birth. Her son, Snorri, is the first recorded European child to be born in North America. In the spring, they continued south until they found land where wheat and grapes grew wild. They started a colony called Hop (possibly in Nova Scotia).

At first, the Vikings traded woven cloth for furs with the First Nations in the area. Soon, however, trade relations broke down. After three years, the Vikings left the colony and sailed back to Greenland.

Later, Gudrid travelled to Rome. At a time when few women ventured anywhere, these trips made her one of the most travelled women of the Middle Ages.

This stamp, showing a Viking ship, was issued on February 17, 2000.

Gudrid's home probably resembled this reconstructed sod hut at L'Anse aux Meadows, NL—the site of the oldest known European settlement in North America.

141

Catherine Schubert

Catherine Schubert: Through the Rockies

In 1862, Catherine Schubert was living happily in Fort Garry (now Winnipeg). Then gold was discovered in the Cariboo Mountains of British Columbia. Catherine's husband, Augustus, joined a group headed for the gold fields. Choosing not to be left behind, Catherine set off with him across the Prairies. Her Red River cart was packed with their three small children on board, along with sacks of flour and pemmican.

They travelled with a group called The Overlanders and soon found the journey more difficult than they had imagined. In the mountains, they decided to split up. One group went down the treacherous Fraser River. The others, including the Schuberts, rafted down the Thompson River. They reached the tiny settlement of Kamloops just in time for Catherine to give birth to her fourth child, Rose.

For the Schuberts, this was the end of the trail. They settled down first in Kamloops and later in Lillooet. In the summers, Augustus set off for the nearby gold fields. But Catherine preferred to stay on their farm. She had already proven what she was capable of.

142

The Red River cart was used by settlers to carry their belongings over long distances. Fur traders also used these carts to carry furs and trade goods.

Tuquliqtuq: Adrift on an Ice Floe

Another woman who made a difference was Tuquliqtuq [tu-rku-LIRK-turk]. She lived on Baffin Island. In 1853, she met an American explorer named Charles Frances Hall. Because Tuquliqtuq spoke excellent English, Hall hired her and her husband, Ipiirqvik [e-PEER-vik], as guides. They travelled together for the next 11 years.

In 1871, Hall set off with Tuquliqtuq, Ipiirqvik, and his crew on a science expedition to the North Pole. Five months into the journey, Hall died. Then the ship got stuck in ice and had to be abandoned.

In order to survive, the crew divided into two groups. The group Tuquliqtuq and Ipiirqvik joined found themselves stranded on an ice floe off the coast of Labrador. For six months, they drifted south. Ipiirqvik and Tuquliqtuq kept everyone alive by hunting and fishing for their food. Finally, they were rescued by a passing ship carrying an expedition of seal hunters.

Tuquliqtuq, Charles Hall, and Ipiirqvik. This engraving was created in England in 1865 to illustrate Hall's book about his travels in the Arctic.

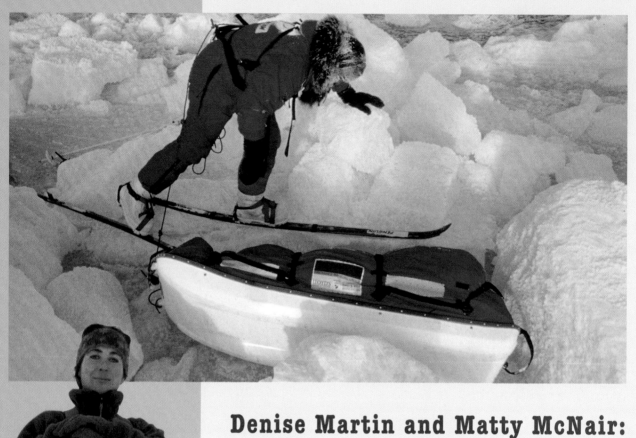

Denise Martin and Matty McNair: Pushing for the Pole

Just over a century later, women were finally in charge of their own polar expeditions. In 1997, Denise Martin from Saskatchewan and Matty McNair, an American, were co-leaders of the Women's Polar Relay. They planned to ski 750 km from Ellesmere Island to the North Pole. Both understood that in the Arctic, as Matty put it, "If you get wet, you die." So they took one-piece, waterproof suits, strong skis long enough to bridge gaps in the ice, and food to feed each woman 5000 calories a day.

The group was divided into five teams of four women. On March 14, the first team with Martin and McNair set out from Ellesmere Island. They would travel one-fifth of the distance before the next team arrived to continue the relay. Martin and McNair skied with all five teams.

The women skied through blizzards. They floundered in soft snow. Some lost ski poles and other equipment when cracks opened before them. But as team after team was flown in, they pushed closer to their goal. Finally, on day 74, Denise Martin became the first woman to reach the North Pole. She and Matty were the only women who had skied the full distance.

Today women climb mountains, photograph life under the sea, and orbit the Earth in outer space. They are following in the footsteps of the early female explorers who led the way.

MEDIA WATCH

Search in magazines, in newspapers, or on the Internet for stories about modern-day explorers. Make a chart to record each explorer's name, gender, nationality, and destination. What do you notice about today's explorers?

DIG DEEPER ••

1. Which expedition did you find most exciting? Why? Give a summary of the expedition to a partner, speaking in the explorer's voice.

2. Describe your dream expedition. Write a journal entry or blog explaining where you would like to explore and why you want to go there.

Step on Board

What would it be like to step into history?

YE *Matthew* LEGACY
June 24 1997

STEP ON BOARD
15TH CENTURY SHIP REPLICA
INTERPRETATION CENTRE • GIFTSHOP

READ LIKE A WRITER

What linking words does the brochure writer use to connect ideas?

In May 1497...

... a small wooden ship called the *Matthew* set sail from Bristol, England. It was destined for the Far East. The Italian explorer Giovanni Caboto (John Cabot) was at the helm with his crew. Caboto, his crew, and their financial backers believed that it was possible to reach Asia by sailing west across the Atlantic Ocean. They were not alone.

In 1474, the Florentine cosmographer Toscanelli wrote a now famous letter to the King of Portugal. In it, he described how one could find Asia by sailing west. Caboto's friend and fellow explorer, Christopher Columbus, also believed that it could be done. In fact, anyone who examined Martin Behaim's 1492 globe could see clearly that east and west were separated by only a short span of sea.

History would prove them all wrong. Within six weeks, the *Matthew* made landfall. The crew landed, however, not in the fabled lands of the Far East, but on the shores of what they called "the New World." Here, they would discover not spices or silk, but cod—an unexpected reward.

John Cabot

Chart a Voyage of Discovery

Today's *Matthew*

The *Bonavista Matthew* is a full-scale replica of Caboto's 1497 vessel. It was built in 1997–98 by a team of seven shipwrights and four carpenters from the local area (near Bonavista, Newfoundland and Labrador). A master builder directed the building of it. Its construction marked the 500th anniversary of Giovanni Caboto's voyage. Today, the vessel serves as a lasting reminder of the voyage and discovery that changed the course of history.

147

How Fast Can the *Matthew* Sail?

The *Matthew* is an example of a 15th century caravel. Caravels were often rigged with three triangular sails, or lateens. On long ocean voyages, these sails were replaced with square sails to make the ship easier to handle and go faster when sailing with the prevailing winds. In favourable conditions, a ship like the *Matthew*, rigged with square sails, could reach a top speed of between six and eight knots. That's less than 15 kilometres per hour.

What Size Crew Did It Take to Sail the *Matthew*?

Historical records tell us that there were around 20 men on board the *Matthew* when it set sail in 1497. This number included Caboto, a barber-surgeon from Genoa, a Burgundian, two Bristol merchants, and at least 14 British sailors.

How Did the Crew Spend Their Time?

As well as the main task of sailing the ship, there was plenty of other work to keep the crew busy. Like most wooden vessels, the *Matthew* undoubtedly leaked. Manning the pumps to remove excess water would have been a near constant occupation. For Caboto and his trusted crew members, there were also sightings and soundings to take and speeds and positions to be determined. When they were not working, sleeping, or eating, crew members probably amused themselves with music, conversation, or a game of cards or dice.

Where Did Everyone Sleep?

There are three cabins aboard the *Bonavista Matthew:* one for Caboto, as captain, and the other two for the barber-surgeon and the boatswain. On the original *Matthew*, it is likely that the merchants on board would have also had cabins. The rest of the crew were forced to sleep anywhere they could find a spot—amidst ropes, supplies and, of course, rats.

Where Did the Crew Cook and What Did They Eat?

Meals were prepared on deck, over a coal fire, if the weather allowed. Main foodstuffs included dried peas, salted meat, and ship's biscuits or hardtack. To drink, there was beer and water. Caboto and the merchants would have provided their own food, including wine, dried fruit, and spices for seasoning.

DIG DEEPER

1. List three interesting things you learned from this brochure that you did not know before. Share them with a partner.

2. Work with a partner to learn more about Caboto's exploration and its impact. Based on this information, role-play a conversation between two crew members about their captain.

Reporters at Work!

What might a radio news report about John Cabot's arrival in North America be like? Of course, radio didn't exist back then, but don't let that stop you! Now it's your chance to create a radio newscast about an important event in Canada's history.

Choose Your Topic

- Select an event related to the early history of Canada.
- List *who, what, where, when*, and *why* questions you could ask about this event and its effects.
- Create an organizer for your information.

Conduct Your Research

- Use a wide range of reliable resources.
- Select information that will answer your questions.
- Look for different points of view about the event.

Write a News Report

- Use your information to write a script for a radio news report about the event.
- Think about how your report will sound when you say it aloud.
- Make sure you answer the 5 W's!

Produce It!

- Work with a group to produce a newscast using your scripts.
- Choose someone to be the anchor to introduce the reports.
- Provide sound effects so listeners can picture the reporter "on the spot."
- Tape your newscast or perform it live for the class.

THINK ABOUT POINT OF VIEW

- Check your sources. Are they reliable? Whose point of view do they give?
- Try to present more than one point of view about the event in your report.
- Include other people's perspectives, but keep your own opinions out of the news report.

H.M.S. *Sapphire* Scuttled!

[SFX: WAVES/PEOPLE YELLING]

REPORTER: I'm here in the Bay Bulls harbour on the southern coast of Newfoundland. It's September 11, 1696. I'm watching the H.M.S. *Sapphire*, a 32-gun frigate. It's on fire and about to sink! The *Sapphire* was in Bay Bulls to protect English fishing interests. Eyewitnesses say the *Sapphire* was surrounded by four French ships. Rather than be captured, the captain, Thomas Cleasby, decided to abandon the ship. Then he set it on fire. I spoke to Captain Cleasby a few minutes ago, and he told me that he believes he made the right decision. If he had tried to fight, lives would have been lost.

[SFX: FRENCH SOLDIERS SHOUTING ORDERS/TOWNSPEOPLE SOUNDING ANGRY]

REPORTER: Meanwhile, it seems the French are taking over the town. Their leader, Jacques-François de Brouillan, announced that the cod fisheries belong to France. Townspeople are not happy that their community was so poorly defended by the English. Now they may be living under French rule for some time to come.

This is Arjun Lafontaine, your on-the-spot reporter, at Bay Bulls, Newfoundland.

[SFX: CREAKING SOUND/PEOPLE YELLING "IT'S GOING DOWN!"]

First Contact

by Nicole Nicholas

How can fiction make voices of the past come to life?

Out of the corner of my eye, I saw something odd creeping over the horizon. I quickly left my fire and hurried to the beach. What was it? I could sense the uneasiness coming from the totem pole watchman. Could the rest of the camp? But Mother told me not to worry—it was just a cloud.

Father's totem pole would watch it. But the cloud started to look even stranger; it looked like the cloud was covered with spider webs—what was it? The adults thought it was a spirit. I heard talk about the spirit of **pestilence**. As it got closer, we began to see people on it. Why would there be people on a spirit? It couldn't be a spirit then…could it be a boat?

The people on the boat were friendly, but we did not know the language they spoke. They did not stay for long. They mentioned the land belonged to them now. What did that mean? Land could not be owned.

About 10 years later, I, much older now, saw another ship coming. I alerted the camp and we gathered around the totem pole I had carved. When these people landed, we did not understand them, either. But it was a different language from before. We began to trade our carvings, furs, and other goods for artillery, utensils, and tools. They came and went for a long time, and we learned to decipher bits of their language, and they, ours. I was sure they would still be trading with us long after my time. After my death, my son, John, will continue…

pestilence
a widespread, infectious disease that can cause death

READ LIKE A WRITER
How does the author use questions to add interest to this story?

153

John

The Russians, as they told us they were called, kept trading until a century passed. We learned all their languages and customs well in this century. Our children became the children of the east. They became peacekeepers and translators for the Elders who did not wish to learn the language of the Russians. The change of youth to the eastern way began the slow disappearance of our history.

No more happens in my time. My son, Charles, will continue the story...

Charles

At the end of the century, more men, from a new country, came and changed the name of our island. We called this land *Xhaidlagha Gwaayaai* (Haida Gwaii), and they called this land the Queen Charlotte Islands. That was the name of the Europeans' boat, the *Queen Charlotte*. Around this time, we had almost 30 000 Haida on these islands, but the fur traders and explorers brought a strange disease they called smallpox. Soon entire camps were abandoned, or the populations died because of all the disease… By this time, there were only 588 Haida left. It was just devastating. I was elderly and very lucky to have been spared.

My daughters, though, were not so lucky. They had settled down with husbands, but the White men wanted them for their wives. When the White men came to take them, my dear daughters felt already gravely ill. But there was a light during this tough time for my people: my daughters did not spread the disease to anyone in camp.

Soon after they were taken from us, we held a ceremony to honour my daughters and their inevitable deaths. Our people lived now as we did before, but much weaker.

Isaac, my son, carries on my story…

Isaac

Since the strange men came to our island long, long ago, we have been becoming more like them. Many of our customs and traditions have been lost. Our traditional clothing, the **button blankets** and our capes, used to be worn at all times; now those clothes are only worn during ceremonies and other special occasions.

We lost our land to the Europeans and were made to live on a small land. We were being treated like we were no longer humans. We were, to the Europeans, not able to do what even the simplest-minded child could do.

I sometimes wonder how life would be different if the White man had never come. How would our culture be? Would it be like it was hundreds of years ago? Would we rely solely on fishing or on animals we hunt in the forests? Would we have been at peace with nature after all these years? Would we still have changed our ways to keep up with the changing world around us, or would we have isolated ourselves so we could stay to our traditional ways? I guess we will never know. I leave the ending of this epic tale to my dear son, Eli…

MEDIA WATCH

Look in newspapers or magazines to find an article about First Nations cultures or issues such as land claims. What different points of view does the article include? How can you tell?

button blankets
wool blankets decorated with buttons and showing family crests

Eli

For this fictional story, 16-year-old Nicole Nicholas won the Canadian Aboriginal Youth Writing Challenge. Participants were asked to write about a defining moment in Aboriginal history.

During my time, a lot of progress has been made. A lot of wrongs have been made right. Our Haida culture is slowly, but surely, creeping back to today's youth. Our strong and proud history is being passed on by Elders through their stories.

In 1960, we were granted our right to be human again; we could decide who ruled what from now on. More people respect us and our history. A past tradition has been brought back to Haida Gwaii—the watchmen. My family has carved watchmen for as long as there were watchmen. I am told, soon I will be able to continue this tradition for my family, as our camp needs a new one.

DIG DEEPER

1. Whose perspective is presented in this story? Whose perspective is not presented? Discuss as a group.

2. Research the Haida watchmen. What are they? What was their significance to the Haida people in the past? What is their significance today? Display your findings visually.

Place Names

Illustrated by Tina Holdcroft

READ LIKE A WRITER
Why did the writer choose to present the information as labels on a map?

Canada's **place names** tell a lot about this country's history. Long before Europeans arrived in North America, First Nations and Inuit had their own names for rivers, mountains, islands, and settlements. Some of these names were adopted by the Europeans and are still used today. In other cases, the newcomers thought up their own names. Some names reveal a lot about the landscape. Others pay tribute to events that happened. Still others reflect an odd sense of humour! Here are a few examples of the interesting stories behind the place names of Canada.

157

What secrets are in a name?

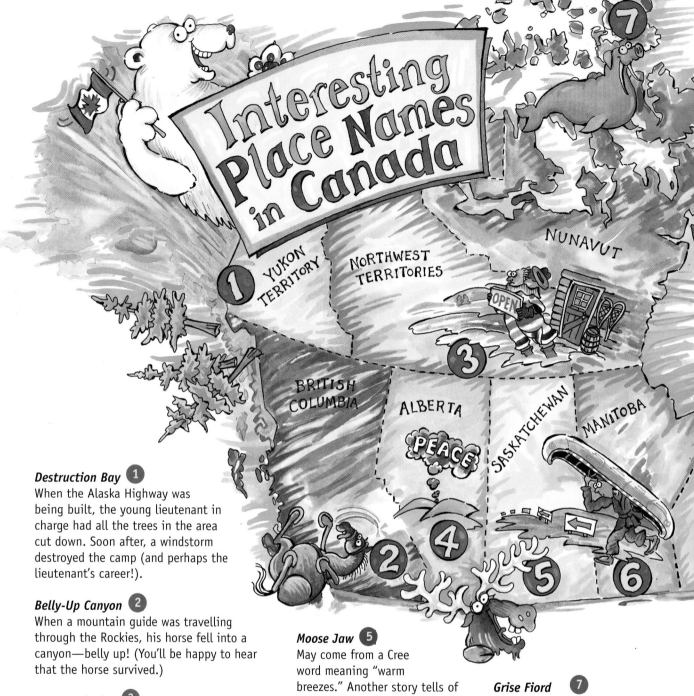

Interesting Place Names in Canada

Destruction Bay ①
When the Alaska Highway was being built, the young lieutenant in charge had all the trees in the area cut down. Soon after, a windstorm destroyed the camp (and perhaps the lieutenant's career!).

Belly-Up Canyon ②
When a mountain guide was travelling through the Rockies, his horse fell into a canyon—belly up! (You'll be happy to hear that the horse survived.)

Fort Resolution ③
In 1815, this was the most northerly trading post owned by the Hudson's Bay Company. Anyone staying at the isolated fort needed to be resolute to put up with the harsh conditions!

Wetaskiwin ④
Means "place of peace" in Cree and "peace hills" in Blackfoot. Around 1860, when Cree and Blackfoot camped on separate sides of a hill, the chiefs met and agreed to make peace.

Moose Jaw ⑤
May come from a Cree word meaning "warm breezes." Another story tells of a broken wagon that was repaired with bones from a moose's jaw. Which version do you prefer?

Portage la Prairie ⑥
First Nations and voyageurs had to carry (or portage) their canoes here to reach the river. It must have felt like they were carrying them across the Prairie!

Grise Fiord ⑦
Grise means "pig" in Norwegian. A Norwegian explorer thought the walruses in the area sounded like grunting pigs!

Pelee Island ⑧
The eastern side is treeless, so it was named Bald Island (*pelé* means "bald" or "bare" in French).

Puvirnituq
An Inuktitut word meaning "it smells of rotting meat."

Cap Diamant
In 1542, Jacques Cartier thought he found diamonds here. The rocks turned out to be quartz. Was he ever ticked off! Since then, "un diamant du Canada" (a Canadian diamond) has meant a trick or scam.

Portage Kamushkuapetshishkuakanishit
One of the longest place names in Canada; a Montagnais word meaning "when we take this portage, we stumble over roots."

Aroostook River
From a Maliseet word meaning "good river for everything." What more can you ask for?

Mistake River
In 1828, lumberjacks followed what they thought was the Sissiboo River. It wasn't!

Witless Bay 14
It's not what you think! In the 1600s, the area was known as Whittles Bay or Whitley's Bay. A spelling mistake probably caused the name change.

DIG DEEPER

1. Create a welcome sign for one of the communities on the map. Choose an interesting shape and slogan.

2. Research the history of other place names in your province or region. Label a map with the names and their meanings.

159

How can a poster open our eyes to different perspectives?

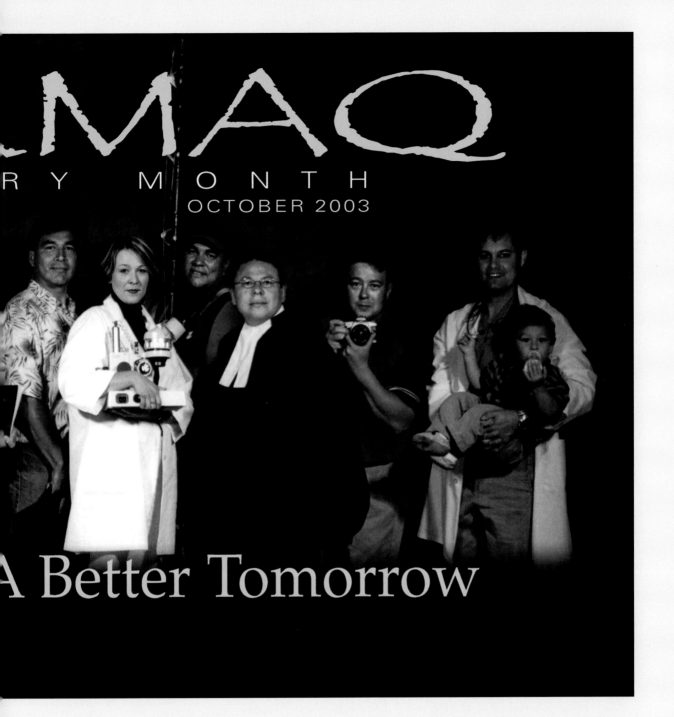

MAQ
RY MONTH
OCTOBER 2003

A Better Tomorrow

DIG DEEPER

1. Why would a poster promoting Mi'kmaq History Month show Mi'kmaq in contemporary roles? Discuss with a partner.

2. Design a poster to celebrate the contributions of Aboriginal youth in your province or region. Include images and a strong slogan.

Northwest Passage

by Stan Rogers

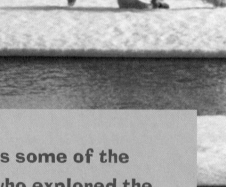

How can songs connect us to our past?

This song celebrates some of the many adventurers who explored the continent and its waterways. Some travelled north to find a Northwest Passage. Others journeyed over land to get from east to west.

Chorus

Ah, for just one time I would take the Northwest Passage
To find the hand of Franklin reaching for the Beaufort Sea;
Tracing one warm line through a land so wide and savage,
And make a Northwest Passage to the sea.

Verses

Westward from the Davis Strait 'tis there 'twas said to lie
The sea route to the Orient for which so many died,
Seeking gold and glory, leaving weathered, broken bones
And a long-forgotten, lonely cairn of stones.

Chorus

Three centuries thereafter I take passage overland
In the footsteps of brave Kelso, where his "sea of flowers" began,
Watching cities rise before me, then behind me sink again,
This tardiest explorer, driving hard across the plain.

Chorus

And through the night, behind the wheel, the mileage clicking west,
I think upon Mackenzie, David Thompson and the rest,
Who cracked the mountain ramparts and did show a path for me,
To race the roaring Fraser to the sea.

Chorus

How then am I so different from the first men through this way?
Like them, I left a settled life, I threw it all away
To seek a Northwest Passage at the call of many men,
To find there but the road back home again.

Chorus

READ LIKE A WRITER
How does the songwriter create rhythm?

DIG DEEPER

1. Which phrases create vivid pictures in your mind? Explain why they are effective. Choose one image and illustrate it.

2. With a group, prepare and present a choral reading of the song. What props or costumes could you use?

I have a confession to make.

READ LIKE A WRITER

How does the author write sentences that sound like a conversation?

Most of the research about Samuel de Champlain is so boring it makes me want to pop my eyeballs out of their sockets and bounce them against the wall. It's just one long list of his comings and goings, hithers and thithers (not to mention his yons).

Samuel zipped back and forth so many times you could think that crossing the Atlantic was as easy as a trip to the local doughnut shop—but I assure you it was not. In those days, the ships were small and tubby. They rolled from side to side like crazy while going up and down, up and down on the waves. They didn't have engines, so they relied strictly on wind power, which meant half the time they were sitting with their sails flapping, and the rest of the time they were zooming along like an out-of-control jet plane, usually in the wrong direction. Also, there were storms. And fog. And icebergs. The holds of these ships were horrible, dark and smelly. People got seasick. Sometimes they died. Food rotted. The smell was…well…ugh. And the journey across the Atlantic took at least a month. So when Samuel tells us cheerfully that he made the crossing 21 times, feel free to reply with a head-slap and a cry of "Are you kidding?"

I can't stop staring at the white foam on this river! It's so much more violent than I expected. It reminds me of the summer of 1610, when Samuel stopped here because his boat couldn't get up the rapids.

How can humour make history come alive?

double-
YOW!

A year earlier, he had joined his Algonkin, Wendat, and Innu friends in a battle against the Haudenosaunee (which many people call the "Iroquois Confederacy"). He did it to seal his friendship with them and to make sure they would stay on his side when trading furs. He felt pretty sure of himself because he had guns and the Haudenosaunee didn't…and as predicted, his side won the fight even though they were seriously outnumbered. Samuel killed two enemy chiefs, and then a third. A gun had never been seen (or heard!) before, and it caused a panic. The End.

It was a short battle. But when they fought again the next year, it was harder to win. An arrow went through Samuel's ear into the side of his neck. YOW! He yanked it out and kept fighting (double-YOW!), but that was the last time he and his allies won against the Haudenosaunee.

After the battle, when Samuel was getting ready to leave once again for France, a teenager in his party (we think it was Etienne Brûlé) kept begging to be left behind so he could spend more time with his Algonkin friends. But in the Algonkin culture, if anything bad happened to Etienne, Samuel would have to fix the balance by taking revenge—and the Algonkin certainly **didn't want that!** Finally, someone came up with the idea of an exchange: a Wendat boy would go with Samuel, and Etienne would stay with Chief Iroquet and his people. Then, at the end of the year (if all went well) they would meet again at the Lachine Rapids and switch back.

So Etienne stayed in North America and had a fabulous time, travelling long distances up the Ottawa River and to the Wendat Nation near Georgian Bay. Meanwhile, the Wendat teenager (Samuel called him Savignon) travelled to France and found that the Europeans were **very strange people** indeed.

In 1611 Samuel came back as planned, to meet up with Iroquet and Etienne and the others. But they weren't here. He checked his Daytimer to make sure he hadn't goofed up the date and then settled down to wait, toodling around in a leaky canoe, touching down on the spot that later became Montreal, and making up some more names for things.

166

Anyway, Samuel's sightseeing and naming spree ended with a terrible shock, right here in this river. One day, Savignon and two friends tried to shoot the rapids, but their canoe flipped over. The other boys drowned, and Savignon struggled back to camp by himself, frightened and exhausted.

Oh no! Here come our life jackets and helmets. And you seem to be putting them on quite happily. Didn't that scary story change your minds? No? Then I must be as brave as Samuel.

When he finally met up with Iroquet and safely exchanged Savignon for Etienne, there was an uneasy moment. A bunch of freelance fur traders had followed Samuel to the rapids, and Iroquet's people were (naturally) suspicious of them. They didn't like these uninvited hucksters, and they couldn't help wondering if Samuel had brought them there on purpose. Talking didn't cut it. Samuel wanted to show Iroquet's people that he was brave and trustworthy. So he agreed to shoot the rapids himself. In his underwear.

Whatever you do, don't let go.

Considering that two boys had just drowned here, and considering that Samuel didn't know how to swim, and considering that life jackets hadn't been invented yet, this was either incredibly brave or incredibly foolish of him. Men from Iroquet's party stripped down and climbed into eight canoes. Samuel, feeling shy, kept his undershirt on and tried to look calm while everyone stood around giving helpful advice, like "IF there's an accident, hang onto that cross-brace in the middle of the canoe," and "Whatever you do, don't let go."

Samuel's friends must have been amazed and frightened by his boldness. But off he went, riding the criss-crossing waves with **his undershirt flapping in the wind**. Luckily, no unexpected rocks jumped out to smash his canoe. No sudden currents tumbled him upside down. No gigantic waves swamped him. By the time Samuel finally reached the bottom of the rapids, Iroquet's people respected him more than ever. His daredevil performance—which was all in a day's work to them, but not to Samuel—sealed their friendship. Later, he wrote that he had been very nervous. Even the bravest person in the world, he said, would not have been able to do this without great apprehension. (He wasn't bragging. That was just a plain fact.)

Later in his life, Samuel did **many other brave things.** But in the end, none of those adventures killed Samuel. When he was sixty-something years old and living a quiet life in Quebec (doing more gardening and less shooting of rapids) he had a stroke that left him paralyzed. He died on Christmas Day in 1635, in his very own bed.

That may be sad, but it comforts me a little as we lower ourselves into this jiggly rubber raft. Perhaps there's a tiny chance we might survive this adventure and die of old age in our very own beds. But first we must be brave, like Samuel de Champlain! Here we go:

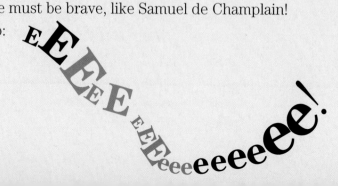

EEEEEEEEeeeeeeeeeeee!

DIG DEEPER

1. Retell the "shooting of the rapids" story from the point of view of Etienne Brûlé or someone else from Champlain's group.

2. Choose another event from Champlain's life or the life of another European explorer in Canada. Draw a four- to six-panel cartoon to describe the most important things that happened. Use speech balloons to show what the characters are saying. Feel free to add some humour to your cartoon!

This Land Is My Land

by George Littlechild

READ LIKE AN ARTIST

How do the author's descriptions help you see the paintings as he sees them?

I Love the Moon, the Stars, and the Ancestors

I paint at night. I'm inspired to paint at night. I stand outside staring at the night sky and I begin to dream. The sky is like a doorway into the other world, the Spirit World.

I am inspired by the ancestors. When I look back on our history and see all the difficulties our ancestors had to face, I can only honour them. Through the wisdom of our Elders and the courage of all our people we have survived the past 500 years. I thank the Creator for *Wahkomkanak* [wah-KOM-kan-ak], our ancestors.

In the centre of this picture is Chief Joseph Samson. He wears an eagle headdress, the highest symbol in our culture. On the top and the sides of the picture are images of my great-great-grandfather, Louis Natuasis, who lived from 1858 to 1926. He was a headman to Chief Joseph Samson. He was born when my people were still free, when the buffalo still roamed.

In those days our Nation, the Plains Cree people, followed the buffalo in the spring and summer. In the winter we made camp by the rivers, which were the ancient roadways. The trees protected us from the snows and the winds. We hid in the valleys from our traditional enemies, the Blackfoot people.

How does the past affect the present?

Columbus First Saw

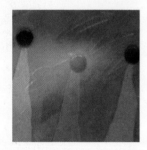

The man in my painting is looking at Columbus and he is totally surprised. I, too, would have been surprised if I had been there. "Who are these men whose skin is so pale? Have they come from the Spirit World to guide us? What do they want, these men who are not like us?"

I remember hearing about Columbus at school when I was a boy. The teacher said he was a great man because he had discovered America. Even then I wondered how Columbus could have discovered America when my people were already here.

Since Columbus came to the Americas, my people have lost most of our land and we have suffered much. Knowing what I do now about our history, I would have offered Columbus a meal and a place to stay and treated him as a guest, but I would not have allowed him to take away our land.

Mountie and Chief

This picture brings you face to face with two different cultures. The Mountie is a Royal Canadian Mounted Policeman sent by the Queen of England and the Government of Canada to enforce the law of the Europeans. The Chief is a leader of the Plains Cree. He is protecting our people and our way of life.

But our way of life was being destroyed. The White men were taking more and more of our land. They put us onto reserves, which were just little pieces of the territory we used to have; and we couldn't come or go without their permission. My ancestors must have cried much as they became prisoners on their own land.

Four Buffalo Spirits

The mighty buffalo fed and clothed my ancestors. Millions of these magnificent animals once roamed the plains. By the end of the 1800s they were almost extinct—killed for money by the White men. This extermination was devastating to my ancestors who depended upon the buffalo for their very survival.

I painted four buffalo because four is a sacred number. These four represent the millions who have died. Four is also a healing number. It appears in all my work. There are four directions, four seasons, four elements, and four kinds of animals (those who walk, those who fly, those who swim, and those who crawl).

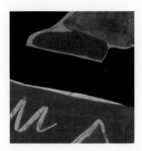

This Land Is My Land

When I was a boy I was taught the song "This land is your land, this land is my land." When I got older, I thought it was very strange to be singing about the ownership of the land. Whose land was this? Did it belong to anyone? The first people in this land were the First Nations. We prefer to be called First Nations or First Peoples, because this was our homeland first.

North America is a very large continent. Add Central America and South America and together they make up the whole Western Hemisphere. This painting reminds us that all this land was once First Nations land.

This Warrior Goes Dancing

This young traditional warrior is on his way to a pow wow. He holds his head up proudly. He's off to go dancing. To dance is to celebrate life. With each beat of the drum we celebrate the heartbeat of Mother Earth.

My people dance at pow wows. We have jingle-dress dancers, who are girls and women. We have fancy dancers, who can be men, women, or children. Boys and men are grass dancers and chicken dancers and do the sneak-up dance. The Elders and the traditionalists dance traditional dances, all together in a large circle.

The circle is a very important symbol to all First Nations because the circle represents strength and unity. When we say the circle has been broken, we mean that our culture has been tampered with. Now we are closing the circle by healing ourselves. We are reviving our culture and traditions. We are very hopeful and the future looks promising.

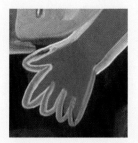

MEDIA WATCH

Think of movies or television shows that portray early life in North America. How are First Nations portrayed? How are European explorers or settlers portrayed? Would you say that these shows are balanced in their presentation of our history? Why or why not?

DIG DEEPER

1. Choose one of the paintings in this selection. Write a journal entry describing what you see in the painting. Then explain your reactions to what you see. How does the painting make you feel? What does it remind you of? When you close your eyes and imagine the painting, what stands out in your mind?

2. Create your own "This Land Is My Land" collage. Include images of people, places, and things that have significance for your personal history or the history of Canada.

Connect and Share

You have learned about the explorers who came to this country and about the Inuit and First Nations living here. Now it is your turn to share what you have learned with your family.

Create a found poem!

- Select a favourite passage from your reading in this unit.
- Identify important and interesting words and phrases.
- Arrange them to create a poem.
- Read your poem out loud.
- Listen to its flow and rearrange as necessary.

Share your poem!

- Ask a classmate for feedback on your poem.
- Take your found poem home to read to your family.

PRESENTING TIPS

- Test possible line breaks by pausing. If it sounds good, it's probably right.
- Try putting key words on lines by themselves.
- Arrange words so they make a rhythm you like.

Spotlight on **Learning**

Collect

- Gather your notebooks, your writing, and your projects from this unit.

Talk and reflect

Work with a partner.

- Together, read the Learning Goals on page 124.
- Talk about how well you met these goals.
- Look over all your work for evidence.

Select

- Choose two pieces of work that you are most proud of that show your learning and how you achieved the Learning Goals. (The same piece of work can show more than one goal.)

Tell about your choices

- Tell why you chose each piece and how it shows your learning.

My choices	I want this in my portfolio because...

Reflect

- What have you learned about making historical facts interesting?
- Why is it important to recognize the writer's or artist's point of view?

181

Acknowledgements

Permission to reprint copyrighted material is gratefully acknowledged. Every effort has been made to trace ownership of all copyrighted material and to secure permission from copyright holders. In the event of any questions arising as to the use of any material, we will be pleased to make the necessary corrections in future printings.

Student Book

Photographs

Cover, i © 2007 JupiterImages Corporation; **v tl** © Bettmann/CORBIS; **2–3** COLUMBIA/MARVEL/ THE KOBAL COLLECTION; **5** © Comstock/ Jupiterimages; **8 l** Canadian Press/AP Photo/Damian Dovarganes, (TV) Photographer's Choice/Getty Images, **c** cbc.ca. Reprinted by permission, **t** Vaughan Public Libraries' Kidszone (http://www. vaughanpl.info/kidszone/funzone/kidsreviews.php), **b** www.brandnewplanet.ca; **iv bl, 10** (clockwise from top) © Car Culture/Corbis, © Pixland/Corbis, © Rainer Holz/zefa/Corbis, Vincent Besnault/ Jupiterimages, Taxi/Getty Images; **11** Amanjeet Chauhan; **13** Amanjeet Chauhan; **15** Courtesy of Jeffrey Probert; **16 t** Photodisc/Getty Images, **b** © LWA-JDC/CORBIS; **17** Ray Boudreau; **23** © Randy Faris/Corbis; **24** © Comstock/Jupiterimages; **25 t** © Blaine Harrington III/Corbis, **b** Ray Boudreau; **26** (clockwise from top left) © Brand X/Jupiterimages, © Comstock/Jupiterimages, © Michael Ochs Archives/Corbis, © Andy Warhol Foundation/CORBIS, © Jason Reed/Reuters/Corbis, THE KOBAL COLLECTION/AMBLIN/UNIVERSAL; **27** (clockwise from top right) © Bettmann/CORBIS, © Douglas Kirkland/CORBIS, © Roger Ressmeyer/CORBIS, Photo by Lionel Hahn/Abaca; **28 t** THE KOBAL COLLECTION/WALT DISNEY, **c** © Catherine Karnow/CORBIS, **b** © Image State-Pictor/ Jupiterimages; **v cr, 29** Mark Van Manen/ Vancouver Sun; **30 t** Reprinted with permission of Junkyard Symphony, www.junkyardsymphony.com, **b** © David Hannan. Used with permission; **31** Luc Beaulieu; **32 t** © Bob Brooks Illustrative,

b Photography Petr Maur; **33** *Maq and the Spirit of the Woods* © 2006 National Film Board of Canada; **34** Purestock/Getty Images; **36 tl** (Rush) © 1989 Anthem Entertainment/All Rights Reserved Courtesy of Rush and Anthem Records, **cl** (Hot Hot Heat) © 2005 Sire Records. Art Direction Steve Walker, Photos Phil Knott, Art & Design Phil Knott, John Hobbs, Stephen Walker, **cr** (The Duhks) © Sugar Hill Records. The Aeroplane, 1957 (collage), Prevert, Jacques (1900–77)/Private Collection, © DACS/ Archives Charmet/The Bridgeman Art Library, **bl** (Eagle & Hawk) Reprinted by permission of the artist, **br** (Neil Young) © 1974 Warner Bros. Records Inc. Art Direction and Design Gary Burden, for R. Twerk & Company, Photography Bob Seidemann, Lettering Rick Griffin; **37 tl** (Eekwol) Courtesy of Rising Sun Productions and Arbor Records, **tr** (Bryan Adams) Photo by Bryan Adams, **b** (Sam Roberts) Courtesy of Universal Music Canada; **62** © Tom Grill/Corbis; **63** Image Source/ Getty Images; **64–65** © Superstock, Inc./ Superstock; **67 and 68** (notepaper and push pin) © 2007 JupiterImages Corporation; **70 c** Reprinted by permission, **tr** Copyright © 2007 North Grenville Public Library. Web site design by Duly Designed, **br** Jacket cover from *Lost in the Barrens* by Farley Mowat. Used by permission of McClelland & Stewart Ltd., Copyright © by Farley Mowat, 1956; **78 t** Digital Vision/Getty Images, **b** Image Source/Getty Images; **79** Ray Boudreau; **95** Digital Vision/Getty Images; **vii cr, 96–97** © AC Fine Art Inc.; **98 tr** Cover from *This Can't Be Happening* Copyright © 1978, 2003 by Gordon Korman. Published by Scholastic Canada.

Shared Reading Posters

Photographs

Illustrations

Text